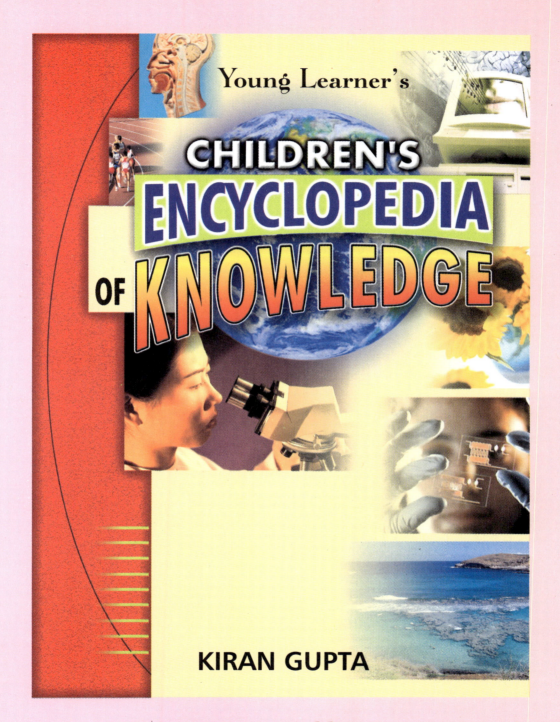

Young Learner's
CHILDREN'S ENCYCLOPEDIA OF KNOWLEDGE

KIRAN GUPTA

Young Learner Publications

G-1, Rattan Jyoti, 18, Rajendra Place, New Delhi-110 008 (INDIA)
Tel : 25750801, 25755519, 25820556 Fax : 91-11-25763428
Website : www.goodwillpublishinghouse.com e-mail : goodwillpub@vsnl.net

I	**LIVING BEINGS** **1-15**
1.	What kind of flowers do the wind-pollinated plants have? 1
2.	What is a virus? 1
3.	What are lichens? 2
4.	How did the humming birds get their name? 3
5.	Why do skunks smell bad? 3
6.	What is photosynthesis? 3
7.	Why are flowers colourful? 4
8.	What is unique about salmons? 4
9.	Why do crocodiles usually rest with their mouth wide open? 5
10.	Which plants eat insects and why? 5
11.	What is chaparral? 6
12.	Is spider an insect? 6
13.	Why are some birds colourful while others are dull? 7
14.	How do the insects help in pollination? 7
15.	What happens to the trees after they lose their leaves in winter? 8
16.	Why do some leaves change colour in autumn? 8
17.	Why do elephants have such big ears? 9
18.	What are fungi? 10
19.	What are nidifugous birds? 10
20.	What are nidicolous birds? 11
21.	What are xerophytes? 11
22.	How is the body of a fish adapted to swimming? 12
23.	Are there any birds which cannot fly? 12
24.	What is the difference between a tortoise and a turtle? 13
25.	What are eels? 13
26.	How are the plant seeds dispersed? 14
27.	Why are the frogs always found near water? 14
28.	How are the bodies of invertebrates supported? 15
29.	How do the fish breathe? 15

II   EARTH AND THE UNIVERSE 16-30

1. Why are the colours in the rainbow always in the same pattern? 16
2. Why does a leap year come after 4 years? 16
3. What does OTE stand for? 17
4. What is continental drift? 17
5. What is a continental shelf? 18
6. What is the internal structure of the earth? 18
7. What is the atmosphere of the earth? 19
8. What is an echo? 20
9. What is an eclipse? 20
10. What is gravity? 21
11. How did petroleum originate? 22
12. What are fossil fuels? 22
13. How are igneous rocks formed? 23
14. How are sedimentary rocks formed? 23
15. How are metamorphic rocks formed? 24
16. How are diamonds formed? 25
17. What is an erratic? 25
18. What are stalactites and stalagmites? 25
19. What is pangea? 26
20. Why is earth the only planet supporting life? 27
21. Why do different places on the earth receive different amounts of sunlight? 27
22. How are different types of weather caused? 28
23. What are earth's vital statistics? 28
24. Why is the sea water salty? 29
25. How old is the earth? 29
26. How are the oceans useful to us? 29
27. How is coal formed? 30

III   ENVIRONMENT 31-46

1. How can the wild life be conserved? 31
2. What would happen if the amount of oxygen increases in the air? 31
3. What is silviculture? 32
4. What is ecology? 32
5. Why does water evaporate? 33
6. What are ecological pyramids? 33
7. Is it true that the formation of Sahara desert is an example of the ill effects of man's activities on the environment? 34

8. What is the ten percent law? 35
9. How are dust particles useful to us? 35
10. Is it true that a dip in Ganga sags the soul instead of purifying it? 36
11. What are the factors which make earth lead in biological revolution? 36
12. What are renewable sources of energy? 37
13. What is environment? 37
14. How does the production of more paper in the world contributes to ecological imbalance? 38
15. What is meant by recycling? 39
16. Why is the use of DDT banned in most of the countries? 39
17. What type of air pollution did the people of London face in 1952? 40
18. What are biogeochemical cycles? 40
19. What is the particulate matter present in the atmosphere? 41
20. What is noise pollution? 41
21. How can we minimise noise pollution? 42
22. What is the cause of the blackening of the marble of Taj Mahal? 43
23. What is meant by the air pollution? 43
24. What are the properties of water which make it a universal solvent? 44
25. What is the role of water in plants? 45
26. How do synthetic detergents cause water pollution? 46
27. What is meant by humidity? 46

IV HUMAN BODY : HEALTH AND NUTRITION 47-59

1. What is a balanced diet? 47
2. What are thrombolytics? 47
3. What is angioplasty? 48
4. What is meant by coronary artery bypass? 48
5. What happens when the heart's own pacemaker stops functioning? 49
6. What are tonsils? 49
7. What is a blue baby? 49
8. What prevents the backflow of blood in the arteries and veins? 50
9. Why do we dream in black and white only? 50
10. Which is the body's largest organ? 51
11. Are all the cells in the human body alike? 51
12. What are the functions of liver? 52
13. What is choking? 52
14. What do the bones do? 53
15. What is our nervous system made of? 53
16. How do the messages travel inside the brain? 53
17. How is food turned into energy? 54

18.	What is sickle cell anaemia?	54
19.	What is substance abuse?	55
20.	Why is it important to burp the baby after feeding?	55
21.	What is Down's Syndrome?	55
22.	What are joints?	56
23.	What is aneurysm?	57
24.	Is the blood always red?	57
25.	Do all the people have the same type of blood?	57
26.	Why do we yawn?	58
27.	What are the teeth made of?	58
28.	What is vaccination?	58
29.	What is meant by atherosclerosis?	59

V   COMPUTERS AND COMMUNICATION 60-68

1.	What is the job of a computer technician?	60
2.	What is the disk operating system?	60
3.	What are Windows in computer terminology?	60
4.	What is word processing?	61
5.	What is desktop publishing?	61
6.	What are bugs in computer terminology?	61
7.	What is meant by processing?	62
8.	What is a menu?	62
9.	What is an input device?	63
10.	What are output devices?	63
11.	What is a virus?	64
12.	What does ROM stand for?	64
13.	What is a byte?	64
14.	What is a bit?	65
15.	What are disks?	65
16.	How should you take care of the disks?	65
17.	Who is a software librarian?	66
18.	Who is a computer sales representative?	66
19.	Who is a systems manager?	66
20.	Who is a technical writer?	67
21.	Who are computer teachers?	67
22.	How is language translated by computers?	67
23.	What is the difference between the Autocad and the Autolisp program?	68
24.	Can our brain capacity be measured in bytes?	68

VI   MODERN TECHNOLOGY 69-81

1. What is a laser? 69
2. What is a lathe? 69
3. What is liquid crystal display? 70
4. What is a loudspeaker? 70
5. What is magnetic levitation? 71
6. What is maser? 72
7. What is a microchip? 72
8. What is a microprocessor? 73
9. What is a metal detector? 73
10. What are monoclonal antibodies? 74
11. What is nylon? 75
12. What is a microphone? 75
13. What is a polaroid camera? 75
14. What is a photocopier? 76
15. What is a prism? 76
16. What is a stereoscope? 77
17. What is a synthesizer? 77
18. What is hydroponics? 78
19. What is glass? 78
20. What is a heat shield? 79
21. What is meant by vulcanization of rubber? 79
22. Why do different aeroplanes have different wing shapes? 79
23. What is a humidifier? 80
24. What is meant by information technology? 81
25. What are jet engines? 81

VII   INVENTIONS AND DISCOVERIES 82-94

1. What was Euclid's contribution in the field of mathematics? 82
2. What were Magdeburg spheres? 82
3. Who invented the television? 83
4. Who manufactured artificial gene in laboratory? 83
5. Who discovered the neutron? 84
6. Who discovered the vaccine for smallpox? 84
7. Who proved that lightning is electricity? 85
8. Who invented the lightning conductor? 85
9. What were Leonardo da Vinci's contributions to science and technology? 86
10. Who gave the internal structure of an atom? 87

11.	Why did Ernest Rutherford receive a Nobel Prize for Chemistry?	87
12.	Who invented logarithm method?	87
13.	Who invented the system of printing?	88
14.	Who invented the germ theory of diseases?	89
15.	Who discovered the law of universal gravitation?	89
16.	Who laid the foundation of the modern theory of evolution?	90
17.	Who invented the first astronomical telescope?	90
18.	Who invented the incandescent electric bulb?	91
19.	Who invented the phonogram?	91
20.	Who discovered oxygen?	92
21.	Who discovered the cell?	92
22.	Who propounded the theory of relativity?	93
23.	Who invented the microscope?	93
24.	What is a telescope?	94
25.	What is Morse Code?	94

VIII SCIENCE 95-106

1.	Why are three digit numbers dialled before the regular eight digit telephone numbers?	95
2.	Why is charcoal a better fuel than wood?	95
3.	What is rusting of iron?	96
4.	How does the water absorbed by the roots in the ground reach the top of very tall trees?	96
5.	What is the composition of sunlight?	96
6.	Why does a steel ball weigh more than an apple of the same size?	97
7.	How does a junk-yard magnet work?	97
8.	What makes moving things slow down and stop?	98
9.	How do the scientists make out that the ozone layer is under attack?	98
10.	What is the principle behind the working of a television?	98
11.	How do hot air balloons fly?	99
12.	How is a hot air balloon steered?	99
13.	What is an echo?	100
14.	What is an electric fuse?	100
15.	Why can't we use a copper wire as a fuse wire?	101
16.	What is dry ice?	101
17.	Why does a ship float while a small stone sink in the water?	101
18.	How is salt obtained from the sea water?	102
19.	What is Pasteurization?	103
20.	Why is the metal body of electrical appliances earthed?	103
21.	What are X-rays?	103

22. Why are X-rays used to study the defects in bones or teeth? 104
23. Why does a person get hurt when he stops a fast moving ball suddenly? 104
24. Why is sodium kept under layer of oil? 105
25. Why does a gun recoil when a bullet is fired? 105
26. Why does a glass tumbler break when boiling water is poured into it? .. 105
27. Why is copper used for making electric wires? 106
28. Who was the first man to set foot on the moon? 106

IX GENERAL KNOWLEDGE 107-120

1. Why are bananas not refrigerated? 107
2. What are Olympic Games? 107
3. What is tele-medicine? Is it useful? 108
4. Which is the most important industry of Assam? 109
5. What does the term paparazzi mean? 109
6. What is an autopsy? 110
7. Which was India's first National Park? 110
8. What is Mach Number? 111
9. What do you mean by consumer bar code? 111
10. What are skyscrapers? 112
11. Which family has won the maximum number of Nobel Prizes? 113
12. What is Koran? 113
13. Which scientist obtained more than 1000 patents in his life? 114
14. What is a rolling settlement in the stock market? 114
15. What is a boomerang? 114
16. What was the Doomsday Book? 114
17. What is the Sphinx? 115
18. What does 'dating' refer to in the stock market? 115
19. What is sky diving? 116
20. What is an abacus? 116
21. Who produced the first animation film? 116
22. What is NASDAQ? 117
23. What makes the Leaning Tower of Pisa lean? 117
24. Who was the first scientist? 117
25. What are tortillas? 118
26. What is Red Cross? 118
27. What is a Nobel Prize? 118
28. What is a black box? 119
29. Which great wonder of the world is found in China? 119

LIVING BEINGS

Q. What kind of flowers do the wind-pollinated plants have?

A. The wind-pollinated plants have small dull flowers without scent or nectar as they do not need to attract insects for pollination. The pollen grains are light and produced in large quantities, so that they get scattered easily over a large area increasing the

Wind-pollinated plants.

chances of fertilization. Their stigma are long and protruding out of the flower so that they can catch the pollens easily.

Q. What is a virus?

A. Viruses are microscopic organisms which cause diseases in plants, animals and man. No chemical spray or vaccine or antibiotics have yet been discovered which can kill virus. They are even smaller than bacteria and whether they are living or non-living is still a mystery for the scientists.

The blue specks in the false-colour scanning electron micrograph are HIV viruses.

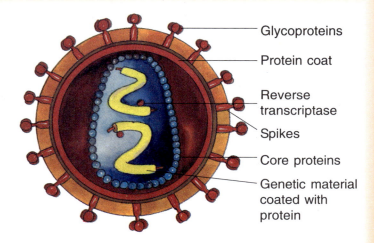

The structure of the AIDS virus.

They can only multiply inside a living cell. They can be crystallized like non-living things and kept for years. But as soon as they are injected into an organism they start multiplying again. They seem to lie on the borderline of living and non-living organisms.

Measles, chickenpox, mumps, AIDS, cold and influenza are some of the diseases caused by viruses in man. In plants, they cause disorders like yellowing and wrinkling of leaves.

Q. What are lichens?

A. A lichen is actually a symbiotic association of two organisms—algae and fungi living together as partners and mutually benefitting each other. The algae prepares food for both while the fungus protects algae from desiccation and intense light. A lichen has little or no roots, leaves or flowers but still they can survive anywhere from deserts to the arctic region. They are slow growing and long living plants. Some grow

Lichens.

as crusty patches on the surface of rocks, trees or walls while others grow as shrubby tufts. Lichens are among the first forms of life that appear after a volcanic eruption.

Q. How did the humming birds get their name?

A. When the humming birds hover over the flowers to suck the nectar, their wings have to flap as fast as 50 times per second to maintain their position. The beating of their wings at such a speed produces a faint humming sound. That is why these birds get the name humming birds although they do not actually hum from their mouths!

Humming bird.

Q. Why do skunks smell bad?

A. The skunks do not smell bad themselves but it is a defence mechanism in them which secretes a smelly liquid. They possess two tiny anal glands at the base of their tail. Whenever threatened they turn around, raise their tail and shoot the smelly liquid onto the face of the enemy. This drives the enemy away.

Skunk.

Q. What is photosynthesis?

A. Photo means *light* and synthesis is *to build*. Photosynthesis is a process by which green plants make their own food in the presence of carbon dioxide, water and sunlight. Oxygen is a by-product of this process which takes place in the presence of chlorophyll. Simple foods like glucose are formed by photosynthesis. They combine together to form complex foods like starch etc. In this process, solar energy is converted into chemical energy.

1. Minerals, water, and other nutrients; 2. Photosynthesis; 3. Energy (ATP); 4. Complex molecules; 5. Sugar; 6. Water; 7. Oxygen; 8. Carbon dioxide; 9. Heat; 10. Respiration; 11. Light Energy; 12. Sunlight
Photosynthesis.

Q. Why are flowers colourful?

A. Flowers are the reproductive organs of the plant containing the stamens and the pistil which are respectively the male and the female part. For seed formation in cross-pollinated flowers pollen must be carried from the stamens of one flower to the stigma of the other. This work is done by insects or birds which get attracted to brightly coloured or sweet smelling flowers. Birds or insects are able to see and distinguish bright colours and visit these flowers for nectar, helping in cross-pollination in the process.

Foxglove.

Q. What is unique about salmons?

A. Salmons can live both in fresh water and sea water. They hatch in fresh water. When they

Salmon.

start growing, they swim downstream and fully grown fish swim to salty water. When it is time to lay eggs, they start swimming upstream and both the male and the female salmons return to the fresh water where fertilization takes place. After spawning, most salmons die.

Salmon.

Q. **Why do crocodiles usually rest with their mouth wide open?**

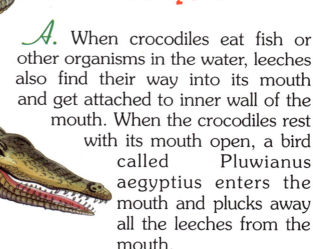
Crocodile.

A. When crocodiles eat fish or other organisms in the water, leeches also find their way into its mouth and get attached to inner wall of the mouth. When the crocodiles rest with its mouth open, a bird called Pluwianus aegyptius enters the mouth and plucks away all the leeches from the mouth.

Q. **Which plants eat insects and why?**

A. Plants like Venus fly trap, Pitcher plant, Bladder wort and Sundew supplement their diet with insects. These plants often grow in wetland areas where the boggy soil lacks nutrients like nitrogenous compounds. To compensate for this, they eat insects which provide them these nutrients.

Pitcher plant.

Q. What is chaparral?

A. Chaparral is a type of vegetation which consists of small trees or large bushes with thick waxy or fuzzy evergreen leaves that conserve water. It is unique to the coastal regions bordering the deserts such as southern California and much of the Mediterranean. These shrubs are able to withstand hot sun or frequent summer fires started by lightning. Although the tops may be burned off, the roots send up new sprouts the next spring. They are very distasteful or poisonous to goats. That is why they can survive even extensive grazing by goats.

The chaparral biome.

Q. Is spider an insect?

A. Although a spider looks like an insect, it is not. Spiders have eight legs whereas the insects have six. Spiders do not have the feelers and wings which the insects have. An insect's body is divided into three distinct parts head, thorax and abdomen whereas a "spider's" body has only two parts combined head and thorax and the abdomen.

Spider.

Infact spiders belong to a different group of animals called *arachnids* which also include mites, ticks, scorpions, etc.

Q. Why are some birds colourful while others are dull?

A. Sexual dimorphism exists in many species of birds. The males have brightly coloured feathers while the females have dull coloured feathers. This is so because the males use their bright colours to attract females for mating while the females are dull so that they can merge with their surroundings while they sit on the eggs in their nests.

Birds.

Q. How do the insects help in pollination?

A. Pollination is the phenomenon in which pollen grains from one flower are transferred to the stigma of another flower through wind, insects, etc. Insects like butterflies and bees visit the flowers to feed on the nectar. In the process their bodies get rubbed

against the anthers (male reproductive parts of the plant) which contain loosely held pollen grains. These pollens stick to their bodies and feet. When the insects visit the other flower, some pollens may fall off from their bodies on to the stigma (the female reproductive parts of the plant).

Insects role in pollination.

Q. What happens to the trees after they lose their leaves in winter?

A. Since the leaves are the food factories of the plant, it is expected that the tree would die after losing all the leaves. But it is not so. The trees remain in a dormant state after losing leaves so that they require less energy. They live on the stored food and survive the harsh winters till the leaves reappear in spring.

Tree in dormant state.

Q. Why do some leaves change colour in autumn?

A. The leaves of the plants are green in colour, but as the fall approaches they turn blue, red, orange or yellow. This happens

The colour of leaves of some trees changes to red in autumn.

because the green pigment or the chlorophyll in the leaves begins to break down. Before the leaves fall, all the chlorophyll drains away from the leaf. The other colours which were already present in the leaf begin to show in the absence of the dominant green colour or chlorophyll.

Q. Why do elephants have such big ears?

A. The ears of elephants are big because of the role they play. Elephants live in forests where the sense of hearing is very important. Big ears can catch more vibrations coming from far off places and different directions giving elephants enough reaction time for flight or fight in case of danger. Large flaps of their ears are used to drive away insects and flies that annoy the elephants. They also serve as fans and help in keeping the elephants cool in hot weather.

Elephant having big ears.

Q. What are fungi?

A. Fungi is a group of simple non-green plants with no true roots, stems or leaves. They have no chlorophyll and hence cannot make their own food. They depend on others for the food. Some live as parasites on living plants and animals while the others feed on the dead remains of plants and animals. There are more than 50,000 different kinds of fungi. The drug penicillin and yeast used in the preparation of bread and pizza bases, mushrooms, greenish moulds on bread, etc. are the examples of fungi. Fungi are natural recyclers which break down dead plants and animals and thus, release materials back into the environment.

Fungi.

Q. What are nidifugous birds?

A. The birds in which the newly hatched chicks are well developed and able to take care of themselves are called **nidifugous birds**. The young ones leave their nest in search of food almost as soon as they hatch. Domestic chickens and ducks are the examples of nidifugous birds. They are also known as **nest-fleeing birds**. The role of the parents is only to guide their young ones for searching food and protect them against enemies and ecological hazards.

Nidifugous birds.

Q. What are nidicolous birds?

A. Nidicolous birds or nest-dwelling birds are those birds in which the newly hatched chicks are helpless, naked, and have closed eyes. They remain in the nests for several weeks under the care and supervision of their parents till they become independent themselves. Parents provide them food, warmth and protection during this time. Sparrows, pigeons and crows are the examples of nidicolous birds.

Nidicolous birds.

Q. What are xerophytes?

A. Xerophytes are the plants which can continue growing even under extremely dry conditions and high temperatures. Some examples of xerophytes are Cacti, Calotropis procera, Zizyphus jujuba, Acacia nelotica, etc. These plants have certain adaptations which enable them to survive in such hot climates.

They have extensive root systems to absorb as much water from the ground as they can. They have either no or very small-sized leaves to minimize the transpiration. The surface of the leaves are generally shining to reflect back heat and their stems are hard, woody and covered with a thick bark.

Xerophytes.

Q. How is the body of a fish adapted to swimming?

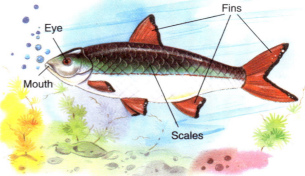

Structure of a fish.

A. The body structure of a fish is well adapted for swimming. It has a stream-lined and laterally compressed body with no protuberances to retard its swift movement in water. Its body is covered with waterproof scales and a mucous coat to reduce surface tension. The fins help in swimming while the tail acts as a rudder for changing directions. Fish have gills on either side of their body, which extract oxygen dissolved in water. The air bladder helps in balancing the outside pressure of the water.

Q. Are there any birds which cannot fly?

A. Yes, there are birds like ostrich, rhea, emu, penguin and kiwi which cannot fly. Such birds are

Ostrich.

Emu.

usually large in size and have long powerful legs for running. These flightless birds have reduced wings, curly, fluffy feathers and a heavy body. Infact ostrich is the largest living bird which can run at a speed of 80 km/h.

Q. What is the difference between a tortoise and a turtle?

A. Although tortoises and turtles look quite alike in physical appearance but turtles are basically aquatic reptiles with limbs modified into paddles adapting to their habitat. The tortoises are land reptiles, which are generally bigger in size than the turtles.

Penguin.

Tortoise.

Turtle.

Q. What are eels?

A. An eel is a long, snake like fish with slender body and poorly developed fins. Its body is like a flat ribbon which in some cases has tiny scales and in other cases it is covered with slime. The eels live in lakes and rivers but migrate to sea to breed. A tiny eel larva called a **leptocephalus** hatches from an egg laid in the sea. It is carried by the currents to the fresh water where it reaches as an *elver* or a young eel. Elvers grow into eels which also find their way back to the sea for spawning.

Common eel.

LIVING BEINGS

Q. How are the plant seeds dispersed?

A. The seeds of different plants are dispersed in different ways. The seeds inside fleshy, brightly coloured fruits are eaten by birds and animals. When the animals defecate, the seeds are thrown out of the body at different places. Some seeds are very light having wing like structures which enable them to travel by wind to far off places. Other seeds have thorns or spines, which stick to the bodies of animals that pass by. When the animals scratch their bodies, these seeds are brushed off to the ground. Coconut fruits have a fibrous coating which helps them to float on water and get carried away to distant places. There are some fruits which suddenly burst open releasing the seeds with great force that they fall far off in all the directions.

Dispersion of seeds.

Q. Why are the frogs always found near water?

A. Frogs have poorly developed lungs. Their moist skin absorbs oxygen and helps them in breathing. To keep their skin moist they remain near the water.

Secondly, frogs complete a part of their life cycle in water. The frogs lay their eggs in water where they hatch into tadpoles. Tadpoles remain in the water, breathing through their gills, till they grow into frogs.

Frogs near water.

Q. How are the bodies of invertebrates supported?

A. An invertebrate is an animal which does not have a backbone. Many such animals are aquatic where the water supports their bodies. Other animals like the stag and beetle have an exoskeleton protecting their body. It is a flexible, hard covering enclosing the body like a suit of armour worn by warriors.

Beetle.

Q. How do the fish breathe?

A. A fish breathes with the help of feather like gills at the back of its mouth on either side of the head. When the fish takes in water through its mouth, it passes over the gills which filter out the oxygen from it. This oxygen enters the bloodstream of the fish and is distributed to the other parts of the body.

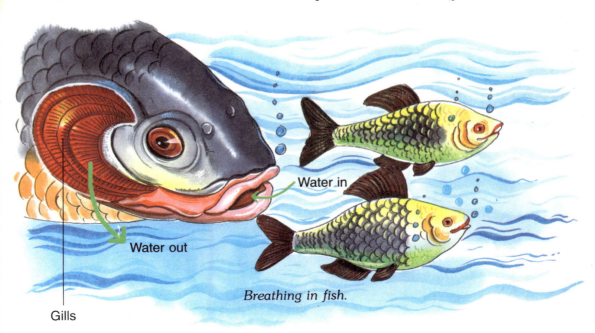
Breathing in fish.

EARTH AND THE UNIVERSE

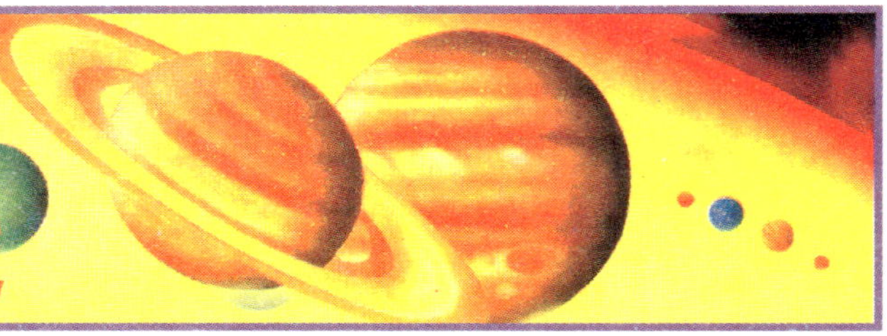

Q. Why are the colours in the rainbow always in the same pattern?

A. When the sunlight enters and leaves the water droplets in air, the various coloured constituents of white light are refracted by different amounts. In the band of seven colours, red colour always appears on the upper side of the rainbow because it is deviated the least. The violet colour appears on the lower side because it is deviated the most. The rest of the colours appear in between according to the amount of their deviations. These colours in the order of their deviations are: Violet, Indigo, Blue, Green, Yellow, Orange and Red (VIBGYOR).

Rainbow.

Q. Why does a leap year come after 4 years?

A. The earth completes one revolution around the sun in 365¼ days. This period of 365 days constitutes one earth year and every fourth year the extra quarters add up to make a year having one more day. This year having 366 days is called a **leap year**.

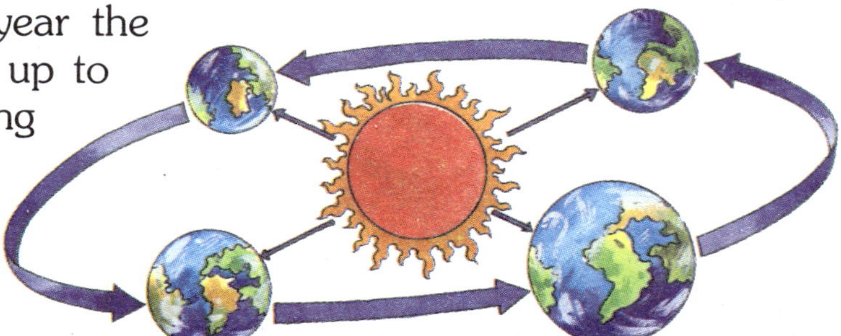

Revolution of earth.

Q. What does OTE stand for?

A. OTE stands for Ocean Thermal Energy. There is always a difference in the temperature between the water on the surface of the reach and in the deeper layers. Sometimes this temperature difference is upto 20°C. The energy available due to this difference is called **OTE** and can be converted into more useful form of energy like electricity.

Q. What is continental drift?

A. The earth's crust and the upper mantle is broken up into huge pieces or plates. These plates float on the semi-molten lower mantle underneath which is heated up by the liquid rocks around the earth's core. Heating sets up currents in the mantle which moves some of the plates towards or away from each other. The plates move the continents along with them. This movement is known as **continental drift** and is a very slow phenomenon. A continent moves only a few centimetres in a century.

As a result of the continental drift, we have the seven continents which were initially together as a single huge landmass.

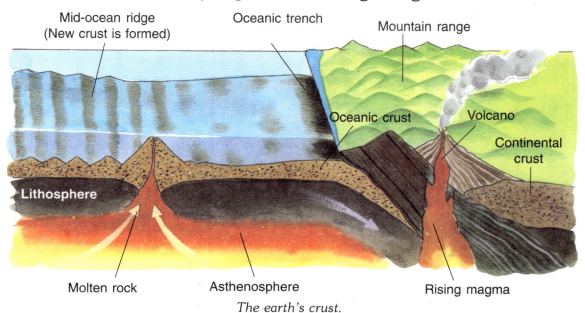

The earth's crust.

EARTH & THE UNIVERSE

Q. What is a continental shelf?

A. The continents do not end where their coasts meet the sea. Their true edges lie far out under the sea. The land under the sea in continuation with the continents slopes gently forming a shelf which may extend upto hundreds of kilometres from the shore. This is called as **continental shelf**. It is full of sea life as it gets enough sunlight. Beyond it lies the deep ocean floor. If the sea level comes down, the continental shelf would get joined to the continents and be a part of them. The British Isles are an example.

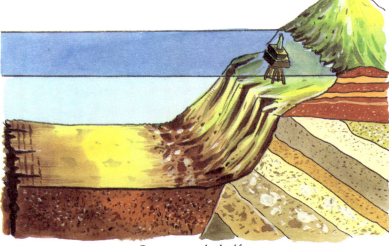
Continental shelf.

Long time back, the sea level was lower than what it is today and the continental shelf was dry land. Studies have revealed the presence of canyons, ridges, and mountains on it which proves that it was once above sea level but has now got submerged under water.

Q. What is the internal structure of the earth?

A. The earth has a definite layered structure with density increasing towards the centre. Its surface is covered with a crust made of solid rocks which may be 30 km thick under the mountains or 3 km thick under the oceans. The earth's crust forms the first layer of the earth going towards the centre. The upper portion of it is called *sial* while the lower portion is called *sima*. A thick layer of hot semi-molten rocks forms the next layer called the *mantle* which is 2900 km thick.

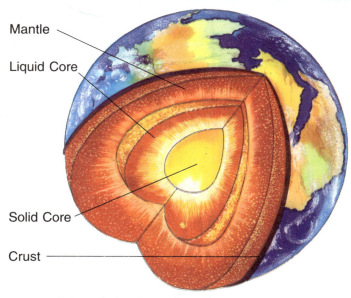

The outer core lies below the mantle and above the inner core. It is 2240 km thick and made up of metals in molten form.

The innermost layer is the inner core which is a 2440 km thick solid ball made up of ferro-nickel. The core temperature is as high as 3700°C and the pressure is 3800 tonnes/sq.cm.

Internal structure of earth.

Q. What is the atmosphere of the earth?

A. The atmosphere is a blanket of air surrounding the earth, held together by the gravity of earth. It consists of a mixture of gases like nitrogen, oxygen and carbon dioxide, which make life possible on earth. It provides the air we breathe. It keeps out sun's harmful rays during the day and stops the heat from leaving the earth at night. The movement

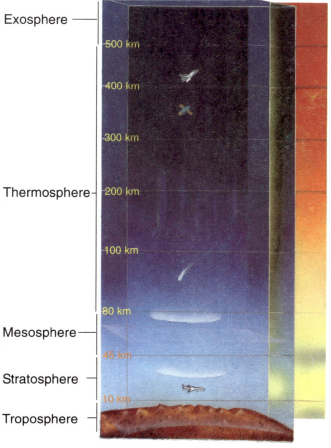

Atmosphere of earth.

of air in the lower atmosphere creates winds which regulate our weather.

The earth's atmosphere is about 32 km thick but it is not the same all the way up. Near the ground it is very dense, getting thinner with the altitude and finally fades away into outer space.

Q. What is an echo?

A. An echo is the sound produced when sound waves are reflected back from an object. There is a time delay between the original sound and the echo. This time delay can be measured.

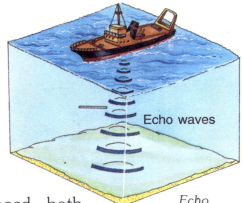
Echo.

Since sound travels at a fixed speed, both can be used to find out the distance of the object reflecting the sound. Ships, submarines, bats etc. use this system of echolocation. A radar also depends on echoes from radio signals.

Q. What is an eclipse?

A. The earth revolves around the sun and the moon revolves around the earth. Due to this they occasionally block out

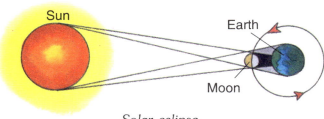
Solar eclipse.

some of the sun's light and the shadow of the earth or moon fall on one another. A solar eclipse occurs when the earth passes

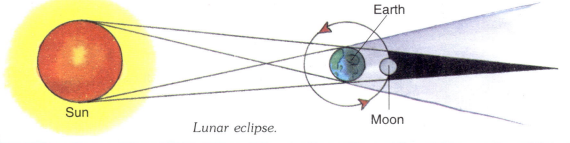
Lunar eclipse.

into the moon's shadow and a lunar eclipse occurs when the moon passes into the earth's shadow.

There are two parts of the shadow. The smaller dark inner shadow is called the **umbra** where total eclipse is seen and the larger outer/lighter shadow is the **penumbra** where only partial eclipse is seen.

Q. What is gravity?

A. Gravity is the pull with which an object attracts other objects towards it. All objects possess this force but big heavy objects like planets, moon, etc. have a stronger force of gravity. Gravity pulls everything towards the middle of the earth. It helps to revolve the moon around the earth and makes all the objects thrown up in the air fall back to the earth.

Apple falls down from a tree due to gravity.

Weight of an object is the force with which the gravity pulls it down. Moon's force of gravity is 1/6th that of the earth. That is why a person weighs much less on moon than on the earth although the mass is the same.

Gravity of earth attracts the objects towards it.

Q. How did petroleum originate?

A. Petroleum oil is formed by the decomposition of the remains of small plants and animals (micro-organisms) that got buried under the sea millions of years ago. The dead bodies of these micro-organisms sank to the bottom of sea and got covered with the layers of mud and sand. Because of the action of heat, pressure, and bacteria on them, they got converted into petroleum oil. The petroleum thus formed got trapped between two layers of non-porous rocks.

Q. What are fossil fuels?

A. Fossil fuels are formed by the decomposition of the remains of plants and animals that got buried under the soil millions of years ago. Coal, petroleum, natural gas are a few examples of fossil fuels. The energy stored in the fossil fuels is actually the

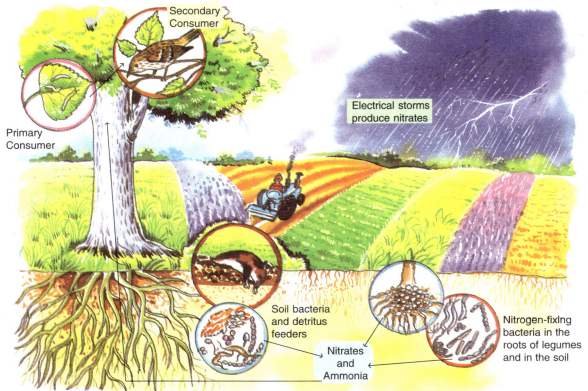

energy of the sun that made the plants grew long time back. Fossil fuels are non-renewable sources of energy. Hence they are very precious and must be used judiciously.

Q. How are igneous rocks formed?

A. Igneous rocks are formed by the cooling of the molten material, either deep within the earth as magma or flowing over it as lava.

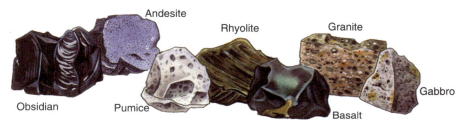

Types of igneous rocks.

When magma cools very slowly deep within the earth's surface, crystals big enough to be seen by naked eyes are formed. Examples of this kind of igneous rocks are granite, gabbro, etc.

But when the lava cools very quickly over the earth's surface, a very fine-grained rock is formed in which the crystals are microscopic. Basalt is an example of this kind of rock.

Pumice is also another igneous rock formed by the action of gases escaping from the surface layers of lava, causing a fracturing of the lava leaving many small holes. It is also formed by the lava flowing under the sea.

Q. How are sedimentary rocks formed?

A. The rocks which are formed by the sediments are called **sedimentary rocks**. Action of wind and rain on the existing rocks withers them to produce small pebbles, sand, silt, mud and dust. These are carried to other places by running water and wind. When they come to rest, usually in water, they settle down and are gradually cemented together forming rocks such as sandstone, gypsum, shale and so on.

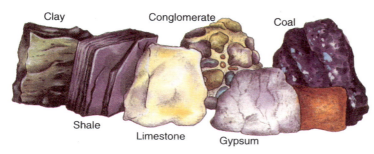

Types of sedimentary rocks.

Limestone is formed organically from the shells of millions of tiny organisms or remains of corals that undergo natural chemical reactions. Chalk deposits are mainly the remains of one-celled animals.

Other sedimentary deposits like coal, oil and natural gas are formed by the compressed remains of plant and animal life that got buried under the soil millions of years ago.

Sedimentary rocks are formed in layers called **strata** and are very useful for the scientists to learn about evolution as they contain fossils.

Q. How are metamorphic rocks formed?

A. Metamorphic rocks are formed by a change in the existing rock from its original state by the action of heat or pressure or by the influence of gases and liquids. Sometimes the change is so small that it is hardly noticeable. At other times it is so drastic that it is difficult to determine the original rock.

Shale is changed into slate by the intense pressure inside the earth.

Limestone is changed into marble by the energy from the intense heat inside the earth's surface.

Sandstone is changed into quartzite while granite into gneiss.

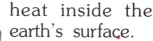

Types of metamorphic rocks.

Q. How are diamonds formed?

A. The kimberlite rock present in the upper mantle at a depth of over 150 km inside the earth consists mainly of carbon. This carbon gets converted to diamond under conditions of high temperature of about 1500⁰C and high pressure of about 70,000 atmospheres that exists at such a depth. When the kimberlite rocks break up in the due course of time then the diamond pieces are brought to the surface of earth where they mix up with the soil. They are hand picked or mined from here.

Diamonds.

Q. What is an erratic?

A. An erratic is a rock fragment which is entirely different in composition from those found in its vicinity. It may range in size from a pebble to a boulder. It may have been transported from its original location to new locations miles away through wind or glaciers. They get carried away frozen inside the glaciers and get deposited wherever the ice melts.

Erratics provide valuable information to the scientists regarding the movement of the glaciers during the Ice Age. The path of the glacier can be traced on a map by determining the source rock of the erratic.

Q. What are stalactites and stalagmites?

A. Stalactites and stalagmites are deposits of calcium carbonate formed in limestone caverns or in other places where water drips continuously. The rocky spikes or icicles hanging from the cave roof are called **stalactites** and the upward pointing spires on the ground are called **stalagmites**.

EARTH & THE UNIVERSE

25

Water which flows through the limestone dissolves some of the calcium carbonate from it and carries it in solution. When this water drips into a cavern, some of the calcium carbonate comes out of the solution as the water evaporates and forms stony deposits which build up and hang as icicles from the roof of the cave. Where the water falls, the calcium carbonate gets accumulated to form a growing pinnacle called **stalagmite**. Sometimes stalactites and stalagmites join together to form columns running from the ceiling to the floor of the cave.

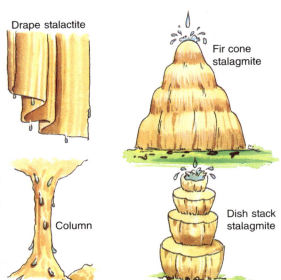

Stalactites and stalagmites.

Q. What is pangea?

A. About 200 million years ago, a big single mass of land comprising all the present continents, existed on the earth. Pangea in Greek means *all lands*. It consisted of all the lands of the earth joined together in one piece. When pangea broke up, the seven continents were formed which slowly drifted away from each other. The evidence can be obtained from the fact that the east shoulder of S. America can be fitted perfectly into the west shoulder of the African continent.

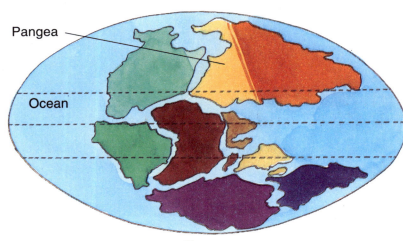

Pangea.

Q. Why is earth the only planet supporting life?

A. The conditions on the surface of the earth and its distance from the sun are responsible for life on earth. Water and the earth's atmosphere together make it possible for a rich variety of flora and fauna to grow here. The earth is at a suitable distance from the sun. Due to this the temperature on earth allows the water to stay in liquid form—both on its surface and in its atmosphere. The earth's atmosphere forms a protective layer of air around the earth keeping the temperature quite steady. The gases like nitrogen, oxygen, carbon dioxide, and water vapour in the atmosphere support life.

Earth.

Q. Why do different places on the earth receive different amounts of sunlight?

A. The earth is not flat but spherical in shape. At any point of time when the earth faces the sun, its rays are more spread out at the poles than at the equator. Also the light rays have to travel farther through the atmosphere to reach the earth's surface from the sun. The poles thus receive slant rays having less intensity of heat. On the other hand, the equator receives direct light of high heat intensity as the rays travel the least and are least spread out on the earth's surface. That is why places near the equator are hotter than those near the poles.

Earth receives different amount of light at different places.

Q. How are different types of weather caused?

A. The uneven heating of the earth's surface creates areas of low pressure at the equator and high pressure at the poles. Because of this, huge masses of air flows between the tropics and polar regions.

Different types of weather.

When cold and warm air masses meet, the air whirls inward in a giant spiral called a *depression* which brings clouds, rain, wind, summer thunderstorms, and even violent tornadoes and hurricanes.

The line where the two air masses meet is called a *front*. When warm air mass catches up with a cold mass, a warm front is created which brings rain or snow. When cold air pushes up behind a warm air mass, a cold front is created followed by showers.

Q. What are earth's vital statistics?

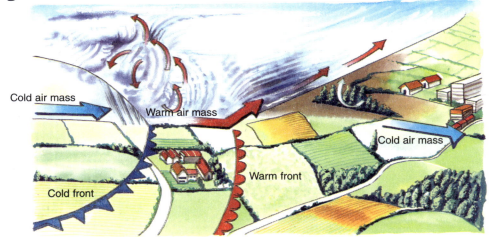

Earth

A. The earth is about 4550 million years old. It weighs about 6000 million tonnes and has a volume of 1,084,000 million cubic km. The circumference of the earth around the poles is 40,000 km while around the equator it is 40,076 km. Its diameter from pole to pole through the centre is 12,714 km while across the equator through the centre it is 12,756 km. The average height of the land is 840 m above the sea level and the average depth of the ocean is 3795 m below the sea level. The area of the water on the earth is about 362 million sq.km (71%) and the area of the land is about 148 million sq. km (29%).

Q. **Why is the sea water salty?**

A. Water dissolves salt present in the rocks while flowing. When this water from streams, rivers, etc. flows into the sea, all the salt along with other minerals are also emptied into the sea making the sea water salty. Also water waves from the sea strikes the rocks along the shores and erode them. Constant withering of the rocks releases salts and minerals which get dissolved in the sea water.

Sea water.

Q. **How old is the earth?**

A. The scientists and geologists have estimated that the age of the earth is between 4–5 billion years by testing the structure of rocks. They believe that the earth first formed about 4.6 billion years ago as a mass of molten matter which has been slowly cooling down over the years.

Q. **How are the oceans useful to us?**

A. Oceans cover about 71% of the earth's surface. In fact primitive life originated in the oceans only. Oceans perform some

Ocean.

very important functions. They regulate the temperature of earth through oceanic and convection currents. They act as reservoirs of sources like sea foods including fish, blue green algae and krill, metals, salts, fossil fuels, etc. They dissolve out the unwanted waste materials of the land and also CO_2 from the air reducing the green house effect. They also act as a medium of transport by boats, ships, etc.

Q. How is coal formed?

A. A fossil fuel, coal is made up of carbon, hydrogen, and oxygen. It consists of the compressed remains of plants that lived about 300 million years ago.

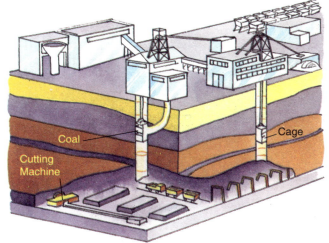

Mining of coal by machines.

When the plants got buried under the soil then a brown, fibrous substance called *peat* formed after a long time. Earthquakes and other changes buried them further and subjected them to heat and pressure. Absence of oxygen prevented further decomposition and pressure from successive layers change the peat into lignite, then to bituminous coal having little hydrogen and oxygen and further into anthracite which is almost completely carbon.

That is why coal is formed in layers or seams under the ground and plant remains can be seen in lumps of coal.

ENVIRONMENT

Q. How can the wild life be conserved?

A. The wild life can be conserved by prohibiting indiscriminate poaching of wild animals, and destruction of forests and their natural habitat. Even if some types of wild animals or birds are in abundance today, their indiscriminate killing should not be permitted. More national parks and sanctuaries should be set up throughout the country and periodic surveys should be conducted from time to time to keep a track of the population of wild species.

Killing of animals should be strictly prohibited.

Endangered species should be given special attention so that they are not lost forever.

Q. What would happen if the amount of oxygen increases in the air?

A. Although oxygen is considered to be a life giving gas, yet high concentration of oxygen in the air is harmful for us. If the amount of oxygen in the air increases, the rate of metabolism of man and animals will become very fast which will lead to harmful effects. More oxygen means rapid combustion. All fuels will burn explosively and it will be difficult to put out a fire. Higher the amount of oxygen, higher will be the occurrence of corrosion of metals, spoiling of fruits and vegetables, and fading of the colours of our clothes.

Q. What is silviculture?

Silviculture.

A. Silviculture is a major programme initiated to replenish the forests by growing more trees and plants. This programme provides raw material for paper industry and at the same time helps in the conservation of wild life, maintaining the water cycle, and preventing soil erosion and floods. It is a great step to improve our environment.

Q. What is ecology?

A. Ecology is the study of plants and animals in their natural surroundings. Scientists who deal in ecology are called *ecologists*. They find out why and how are plants and animals specialized for their habitat, how we can make

Study of animals.

the best use of land, how do the food chains and food webs operate, how can the soil, forests, etc. be properly consumed and so on. These things help to conserve wild life in the nature reserves and also help us to understand the inter-relationship between the plants, animals and nature.

Study of plants.

Q. **Why does water evaporate?**

A. Evaporation is the process of conversion of a liquid into its gaseous form. Two types of forces act on the molecules of liquid. One is cohesive force which holds the molecules together. The other is the motion of the molecules which makes them fly apart from each other. When these two forces nullify each other, the liquid remains a liquid.

Evaporation.

But if the heat is supplied to the molecules of a liquid, then the motion of the molecules at the surface of the liquid becomes more than the cohesion between them and they fly apart from each other. A liquid is said to evaporate then.

Q. **What are ecological pyramids?**

A. The various food chains of living organisms in a community can be represented graphically by drawing pyramids known as *ecological pyramids*. The flow of energy in an ecosystem can be studied through ecological pyramids as they depict the food chains graphically.

The base of an ecological pyramid is very broad representing the producers i.e. plants. As we go higher in the pyramid, it becomes thinner, indicating the successive trophic levels in the food chain. An imbalance in any part of the pyramid necessitates the adjustment of the rest of it.

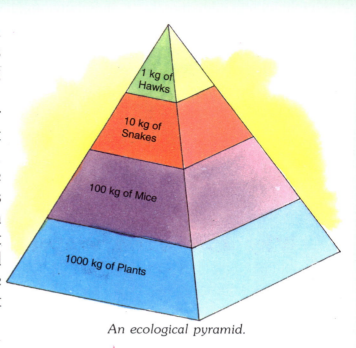

An ecological pyramid.

Q. **Is it true that the formation of Sahara desert is an example of the ill effects of man's activities on the environment ?**

A. Yes, it is unfortunately true that the formation of Sahara desert is the result of man's interference with the environment. When the Romans hunted lions for their sport, the population of lions in the forests decreased rapidly. This in turn led to an increase in the population of herbivores like deer, goats, wild buffaloes, etc. These herbivorous animals ate up all the vegetation and gradually turned lush green forests into vast desert— the Sahara desert.

Sahara desert.

Q. What is the ten percent law?

A. We all know that there is a transfer of energy through the successive trophic levels in a food chain. But no transfer of energy is 100% i.e. some energy is lost at each step. Kindemann

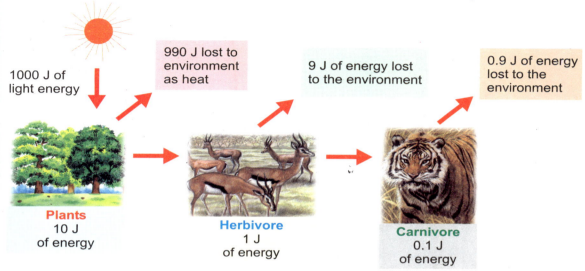

10% of the energy is transferred to next tropic level

gave the 10% law in 1942 which states that only 10% of the energy entering a particular trophic level is transferred to next higher trophic level. So there is a gradual decline in the amount of energy at each successive trophic level as the energy available at each level is only ten percent of the previous level. The rest is lost to the environment as heat.

Q. How are dust particles useful to us?

A. Although dust is a nuisance in the house yet it helps to make the world more beautiful. Dust particles in the upper atmosphere reflect the sun's rays and different colours of the sunlight are scattered over the sky. The coloured sky at the dawn and twilight is due to the dust particles present in the sky.

Dust particles also bring rain. The water vapour taken along with the rising warm air into the upper layers of atmosphere condenses on these dust particles to form cloud droplets. These droplets condense together and fall down to the earth as rain.

Q. Is it true that a dip in Ganga sags the soul instead of purifying it?

A. Ganga has become so much polluted over the years that a dip in it no longer purifies the body and soul. This large scale pollution of the river Ganga has been caused by the discharge of sewage, industrial wastes, synthetic detergents and chemical fertilizers into the river. Even the waters of Ganga are coloured at some places because of the impurities dissolved in it.

Pollution

Q. What are the factors which make earth lead in biological revolution?

A. Even though all the planets like Mercury, Venus, Earth and Mars are made up of the same elements, yet we find life only on Earth. Earth is at the right distance from the Sun, neither too close nor too far. It has the right mass to make sure there is an ocean of water on it to support life. It has the right amount of mass

Solar system.

which influences the right amount of gravitational field to hold back a layer of atmosphere thick enough to support life.

Q. What are renewable sources of energy?

A. Sources of energy which can be replenished by nature over a period of time are called *renewable sources* of energy. Wood, water, air and sun are renewable sources of energy. Renewable sources of energy are less costly and pollution free. But they

Renewable sources of energy.

should be used at the same rate at which they are being replenished otherwise an ecological imbalance is created.

Q. What is environment?

A. The physical and biological world where we live is called our *environment*. Its three main components are : the physical surroundings, living organisms and the meteorological or climatic factors. The physical surroundings include soil, water and air. The plants, animals, and micro-organisms like bacteria, fungi etc. constitute the living organisms. The meteorological factors include sunlight, temperature, pressure, rainfall, etc.

Environment.

Environment is not just a single factor but a combination of all these factors. One of the main factors for the difference in the environment of different places is the effect of human activity.

Q. How does the production of more paper in the world contribute to ecological imbalance?

Cutting of trees for producing paper.

A. The basic raw material used for making paper comes from trees which have to be cut down. For more paper, more trees have to be cut down. Reducing the trees means reduced rainfall, loss of fertile top layer of the soil, destruction of the habitat of wild animals and birds, all of which lead to an ecological balance. Also the by-products of paper industry cause air and water pollution.

Q. What is meant by recycling?

A. Recycling is the process in which used materials are saved and processed again so that they can be used once more. These days newspaper, glass, cans and organic materials are recycled. The use of cow dung for the preparation of gobar gas and the use of compost in the fields are excellent examples of recycling of biodegradable wastes in nature.

Made by recycled material.

Recycling solves the problem of disposing off the wastes because they are being recycled and the problem of continuous and growing demand for the raw materials is also solved because the need for the raw materials reduces as the old materials are recycled.

Q. Why is the use of DDT banned in most of the countries?

A. DDT is a non-biodegradable substance. It cannot be broken down into less toxic substances by micro-organisms. So it becomes a major pollutant in the environment and can be passed along the food chain from the crops to man. Its intensity is increasing and becoming more harmful with every higher step of the food chain. That is why its use is banned in most of the countries.

Use of DDT is banned.

Q. What type of air pollution did the people of London face in 1952?

A. A dense cloud of smog, covered London in 1952 causing the death of about 4000 people. This smog contained sulfur dioxide, a poisonous and choking gas released in the smoke from industries and automobiles. The smog remained over the city for about five days and caused serious respiratory and heart related problems in many people besides killing thousands of them.

Air pollution.

Q. What are the biogeochemical cycles?

A. The circulation of chemical nutrients between the biological world and the physical world is known as *biogeochemical cycle*. It is so called because all the biological, geological and chemical factors are involved. There are four important biogeochemical cycles : carbon cycle, nitrogen cycle, oxygen cycle, and water cycle. In this cycle, the chemical nutrients like carbon, hydrogen, nitrogen, oxygen, calcium and water are absorbed by the plants from soil,

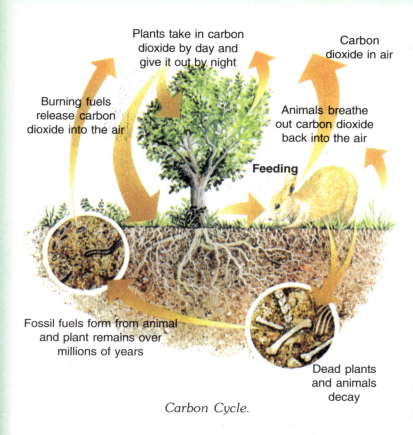

Carbon Cycle.

air or water and are used to make food. Food which gets stored in the body of these plants as chemical energy is transferred to herbivores and carnivores through the food chain. When they die and their bodies decompose, these elements are put back into the soil for circulation through re-absorption by plants. In this way the mineral cycle or the biogeochemical cycle starts again.

Q. What is the particulate matter present in the atmosphere?

A. Particulate matter refers to the finely divided particles suspended in the air. It can be solid or liquid like dust, smoke, fumes, pollen grains, fungi, fur, hair, sand, pesticides, cement dust, lead dust, mist and spray.

These particulates reduce the visibility, pollute the air, cause various allergic reactions and respiratory diseases in man and blacken the buildings and clothes.

Q. What is noise pollution?

A. Any disturbance in our environment produced by undesirable loud sounds is called *noise pollution*. It is produced by machines in the industries and factories, automobiles, aircrafts, railways, electrical gadgets at home, loudspeakers, music systems etc. Unwanted harsh noise is annoying and uncomfortable to us. It also interferes with speech, damages the hearing capacity,

Noise pollution.

and reduces concentration. Loud noises are harmful to patients of nervous tension, blood pressure, and heart trouble.

In this modern age, it is difficult to remove the noise pollution completely but it is possible to reduce it.

Q. How can we minimize the noise pollution?

A. The intensity of noise can be reduced to minimize its harmful effects. Use of loudspeakers and amplifiers should be restricted and music systems should be played at low volume. Machines should be maintained properly so that they make less noise and factories should be set up away from the cities. Vehicles with better designed engines should be promoted. Trees planted along the roads reduce noise pollution. Silencers and ear plugs can be used to reduce the loudness of noise.

Noise pollution can be reduced.

Q. What is the cause of the blackening of the marble of Taj Mahal?

A. Acidic gases like sulphur dioxide and nitrogen dioxide released from the Mathura oil refinery and other industries are the reason behind the blackening of the marble of Taj Mahal. These gases dissolve in the water vapours present in the air to form acid rain. Then this rain falls on the marble. It reacts with marble and corrodes it slowly. The result is the blackening of the marble.

Blackening of Taj Mahal.

Q. What is meant by the air pollution?

A. Any undesirable change in the physical, chemical or biological characteristics of air is called *air pollution*. It may be caused by natural processes like gases released from volcanic eruption, methane gas produced by bogs, pollen grains from flowers, dust raised from dust storms etc. or due to human activities.

Air pollution.

The major cause of pollution is the vehicles, factories, railway engines, aeroplanes, thermal power stations which emit smoke. Gases like oxides of sulphur and nitrogen, benzene vapours, CFCs, etc. are also released as a result of human activities which leads to pollution.

Q. **What are the properties of water which make it a universal solvent?**

A. The water molecules have a polar nature, i.e., one end of the molecule has a positive charge and the other has a negative charge. Due to this, electrovalent compounds like sodium chloride, copper sulphate etc., dissolve easily in water. The ability of water to form hydrogen bonds with the molecules of many covalent compounds makes it possible to dissolve sugar, urea, ammonia, and alcohol. Water also has the ability to dissolve many elements and compounds by undergoing chemical reactions with them and form their solution. For example, water dissolves sulphur dioxide gas to form sulphurous acid.

All these properties of water make it a universal solvent.

Q. What is the role of water in plants?

A. Water plays an important role in the life of plants. It helps in the germination of seeds by softening the seed coat. It also helps in the growth of plants. Plants absorb water and nutrients dissolved in it to grow and manufacture food. Water acts as a medium for

Role of water in plants.

the transport of nutrients from one part of the plant to the other. It gives firmness and structure to the plants by providing the right amount of pressure to the plant tissues. Water also provides a habitat to large number of aquatic plants such as phytoplanktons which include photosynthetic protists, bacteria and algae.

Q. How do synthetic detergents cause water pollution?

A. Though synthetic detergents are better than soaps but they are not biodegradable and hence their excessive use should be discouraged. They cause water pollution because they are not easily broken down into non-toxic substances. They remain in the water for a long time and enter the living organisms through the food chain. They also make the water unfit for drinking and encourage algal blooms in the water bodies. These dense population of algae deoxygenates the water. The aquatic organisms are deprived of the life giving oxygen and they die. This disturbs the balance of the aquatic ecosystem.

Q. What is meant by humidity?

A. Humidity is the measure of the water vapour present in the air. Humidity is low if the air contains a little amount of water vapour and *vice versa*. Warm air can hold more moisture than cold air. On hot humid days, we feel uncomfortable because the sweat does not evaporate easily due to high vapour content in the air. But even too low humidity is not good for us because then we lose too much water and salts from our body.

Humidity of the air can be measured by an instrument called *hygrometer*. Absolute humidity is the actual amount of the water vapour in the air, i.e., the mass of water in a cubic metre of gas. Relative humidity is the ratio of the water vapour present in the atmosphere to the amount of water vapour needed to saturate air at the same temperature and pressure.

HUMAN BODY : HEALTH AND NUTRITION

Q. What is a balanced diet?

A. A balanced diet is a diet which consists of all the essential nutrients like carbohydrates, fats, proteins, minerals and vitamins, water, and roughage required for the normal growth and development of the body in their right amount. No food alone can provide all these nutrients. So, a balanced diet consists of a number of food items. It also depends on the age, profession, state of health of a person and special needs like pregnancy and lactation. A growing child and a lactating mother need more proteins, a man indulging in hard physical work requires more carbohydrates and fats and a convalescing patient requires more of proteins, minerals and vitamins in his diet.

Balanced diet.

Q. What are thrombolytics?

A. Thrombolytics are the drugs which have the ability to dissolve a clot that is blocking the passage of blood in a blood vessel. Such drugs are very effective in treating heart attack caused by thrombosis but are

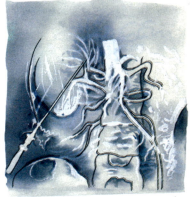

X-ray of an aortic vein with a blood clot.

47

successful only if given immediately, within the first few hours of the attack. This drug can reopen the artery and help to reduce the amount of muscle death.

Q. What is angioplasty?

A. Angioplasty is a technique by which a narrowed artery is widened with the help of a balloon to enable the easy flow of blood through it and reduce the pain. A long tube or catheter with a balloon at its tip is inserted into the heart and guided into the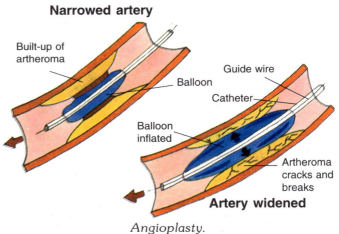

Angioplasty.

narrowed part of the artery with the help of an X-ray monitor. The balloon is then inflated to about 1/10 inch in diameter. It results in the breaking up of the lumps in the arterial wall into smaller less harmful pieces and widening up of the arterial wall at the same time.

Q. What is meant by coronary artery bypass?

A. Coronary artery bypass is an open heart surgery in which diseased and narrowed coronary arteries are bypassed by less essential blood vessels from elsewhere in the body like legs or mammary glands. In this operation, the transplanted vessels are stitched in place alongside the narrowed coronary arteries and they take over the function of the diseased arteries.

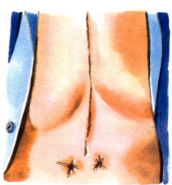

A few days after a bypass.

Q. What happens when the heart's own pacemaker stops functioning?

A. If the heart's own pacemaker stops functioning, an artificial pacemaker about the size of match box can be implanted in the skin and the muscle of the chest near the shoulder. It is a waterproof metal case which contains electronic signal-generating circuit and a battery which lasts up to ten years. A lead from it carries the signals to the heart via a vein into the heart's ventricle.

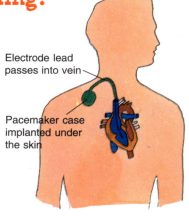
Pacemaker.

Q. What are tonsils?

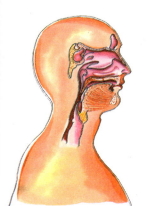
Tonsils.

A. Tonsils are a pair of small lumps of lymphoid tissue at the back of the throat, one on each side of the root of the tongue. They protect the body against the germs entering through the mouth. Their size is very large in children but they gradually shrink and become smaller as we grow old.

Inflammation of tonsils is called *tonsillitis*. In this state they are enlarged and painful. It becomes difficult to swallow also. The doctors may take out the tonsils in such cases as their removal does not seem to harm the body in any way.

Q. What is a blue baby?

A. In new born babies born with a hole in their heart, the deoxygenated blood does not reach the lungs for oxygenation but continues to flow around the body. This causes the baby's skin

Blue baby.

49

to turn blue as its body parts are not able to receive enough oxygen. Such a baby is referred to as **blue baby**.

Q. What prevents the backflow of blood in the arteries and veins?

A. One-way valves present in the heart, main arteries and veins prevent the backflow of the blood. These valves are made up of a pair or more of fibrous flexible flaps of tissues which ensure that the blood flows in one direction only. As the blood is pumped through them in the right direction, the flaps are pressed against the wall so that the blood can flow through them easily. When the heart refills again, the blood tries to flow back into the heart which opens the flaps and makes them bulge together to block the passage.

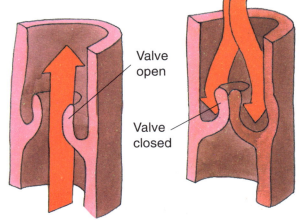

Valves prevent the backflow of blood.

Q. Why do we dream in black and white only?

A. The retina of the human eye consists of two types of cells — rods and cones. The cone-shaped cells are sensitive to bright light and can detect colour while the rod-shaped cells are sensitive to dim light and are used for black and white vision. During sleep, we cannot see through the eyes but our brain is fully

Dreams are black and white.

active. The images enter the brain without passing through light sensitive cone cells and the brain has no cells of its own to differentiate colours. So, we see only black and white pictures formed when rod-shaped cells pass messages along with the optic nerve to the brain.

Q. Which is the body's largest organ?

A. The skin is the body's largest organ. It forms the body's protective covering keeping dust, germs, harmful sunrays from entering the body. The surface area of an adult skin is about 22 square feet and its weight is about 6-7 pounds.

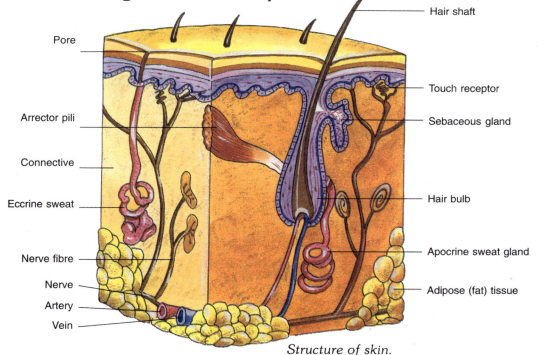

Structure of skin.

Q. Are all the cells in the human body alike?

A. No, all the cells in the human body are not alike. They are of

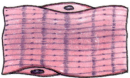

Striped muscle cells

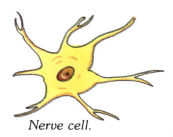

Nerve cell.

different types and shapes depending upon their functions. Nerve cells are long and branched at the top because they carry messages to the brain. The red blood cells are disc shaped because they carry oxygen.

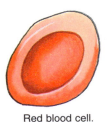
Red blood cell.

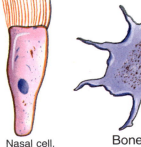
Nasal cell.

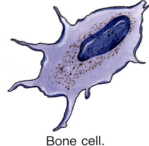
Bone cell.

Types of cell.

Other cells may be spindle shaped, round or irregular in shape.

Q. What are the functions of liver?

A. Liver is an important organ of the body present in the abdominal cavity. It aids in digestion by manufacturing bile juice and also acts as a storage area for glucose which is released in case of need. Its other functions include regulation of blood glucose levels, synthesis of blood proteins, storage of iron and certain vitamins, conversion of toxic ammonia into urea and detoxification of other harmful substances like nicotine and alcohol.

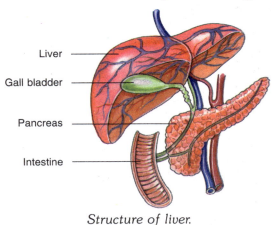
Structure of liver.

Q. What is choking?

A. Choking is a situation when the airway of a person gets blocked so that the person cannot breathe or speak. It is a serious condition because lack of oxygen can result in cardiac arrest and death. Assistance to such a person should be offered immediately.

Choking.

Q. What do the bones do?

A. Bones form the basic framework or the skeleton on which our body is supported. The skeleton gives shape and size to our body. It also protects the delicate organs of our body from injury and shock. For example, the rib cage protects the lungs, the skull protects the brain and the eyes.

Q. What is our nervous system made of?

A. The group of body organs consisting of the brain, spinal cord, and nerves that control and regulate all body activities and functions together constitute the nervous system. The nerves are spread throughout the body in an orderly way and they bring and carry messages to and from the brain. The nervous system especially the brain has a large vascular supply so that it can carry out its functions.

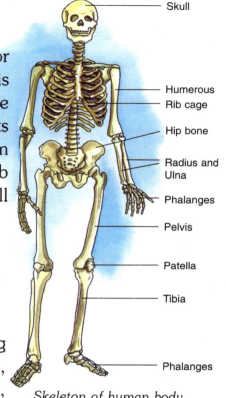

Skeleton of human body.

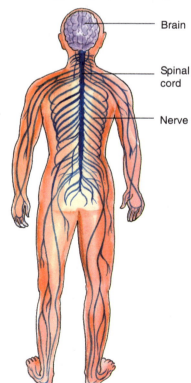

Nervous system.

Q. How do the messages travel inside the brain?

A. There are billions of nerve cells or neurons in the brain which are connected

HUMAN BODY

to each other. Each neuron has many branches called *dendrites* to make contact with the other neurons. Messages are carried along these nerve cells and passed to the other cells connected with them.

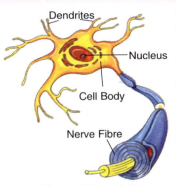

Neuron (Nerve Cell)

Q. How is food turned into energy?

A. When we eat food, it is broken down into smaller pieces in our mouth and is digested in stomach and intestines. Absorption starts in the intestines and from here the food enters the blood stream. Blood carries the food and oxygen absorbed in the lungs by it to different parts of the body by the pumping action of the heart.

Food is burned in the muscles using oxygen by a process called *respiration*. This releases energy and carbon dioxide. The carbon dioxide is exhaled out and the energy is used to do work.

Q. What is sickle cell anaemia?

A. Sickle cell anaemia is a disease caused by a single amino acid substitution in the haemoglobin molecule. As a result the disc-shaped red blood cells get converted into longer sickle-shaped cells greatly reducing their oxygen carrying capacity. These sickle-shaped cells are more fragile than round red blood cells and are thus more likely to break and clog the capillaries.

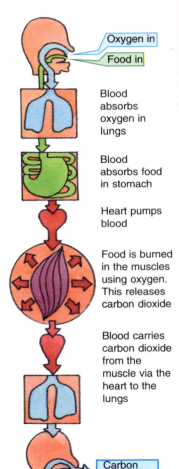

Process of turning food into energy.

The tissues downstream from such clogged capillaries do not receive oxygen or have their wastes removed. This can cause pain and even fatal strokes or heart attacks.

Q. What is substance abuse?

A. Substance abuse refers to the excessive use of mood-altering drugs like alcohol, cocaine, tobacco or caffeine that bring about a negative effect in the person's life. He/she soon becomes an addict of these things and slowly his/her requirement for the drug increases. Finally, the habit of drug abuse controls his/her life.

Family and friends should give an understanding and non-judgemental approach to the patient and help him/her to get out of the habit as treatment for this is available.

Q. Why is it important to burp the baby after feeding?

A. Most infants, especially those who are bottlefed, swallow some air while drinking milk. This air can collect in the stomach and cause uneasiness, vomiting or abdominal pain in the child. That is why it is necessary to burp the body after feeding.

Burping the baby.

Q. What is Down's Syndrome?

A. Down's Syndrome is a genetic disorder caused by the presence of three copies of 21 chromosome.

Children with trisomy 21 or Down's Syndrome are both physically and mentally defective with distinct characteristics like small mouth held partially open, widely placed eyes, distinctively shaped eyelids, protruding tongue, weak muscle tone, etc.

Down's Syndrome.

Much more serious defects include low resistance to infectious diseases, heart malformations, mental retardation, etc.

Q. What are joints?

A. The places where the bones meet in the body are called *joints*. In our body there are some immovable joints like in the skull and some movable joints

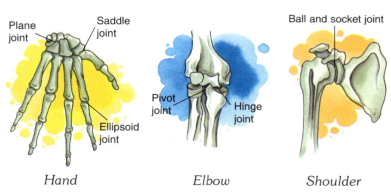

Different types of joints.

like in the hand, legs, etc. There are different types of joints in our body like hinge joint (knees, elbows) and ball and socket joint (hip, shoulder). Strong flexible tissues called *ligaments* hold the bones together and the ends of the bones are capped with rubbery cartilage which cushions the shock caused by movement. Different types of joints help a person to make different kinds of movements.

Q. What is aneurysm?

A. An aneurysm is a localized dilation or bulging in an artery occurring because the arterial wall is thin and weak. It can occur anywhere but is most troublesome when it is in a cerebral artery or aorta. The pressurized flow of the blood gradually stretches the swelling and it may burst also. Blood may flow out between the artery lining and its muscular outer wall and may clot forming embolus.

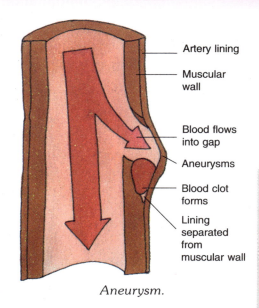

Aneurysm.

Q. Is the blood always red?

A. Oxygenated blood is bright red in colour whereas deoxygenated blood is bluish purple in colour. Red blood is found in the arteries while bluish purple blood is found in the veins.

Q. Do all the people have the same type of blood?

A. There are four different types of blood groups A, B, AB, and O. A person may have any one of these four types of blood. Apart from these, there is a Rh or Rhesus factor also. A person having this factor is called *Rh positive* and a person lacking it is called *Rh*

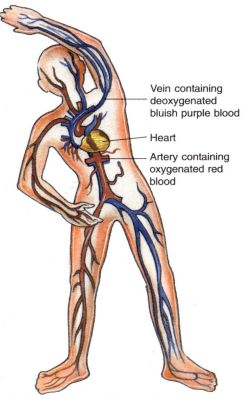

Colour of blood in veins and arteries.

negative. So if a person's blood group is A, he may be A+ve or A–ve depending upon the presence or absence of this factor.

Q. Why do we yawn?

A. Sometimes there is a lack of oxygen in the air due to shallow breathing. This decreases the level of oxygen and increases the level of carbon dioxide in the blood. When this happens, the body responds by taking in an extra breath of air which gets rid of the extra carbon dioxide and allows the lungs to get more oxygen.

Yawning.

Q. What are the teeth made of?

A. The teeth have a layered structure. The innermost core of the tooth called the *pulp* is a soft tissue filled with blood vessels and nerves. Surrounding the pulp is the middlehard bone-like layer called *dentine*. The next and the outermost layer is the enamel which forms a hard

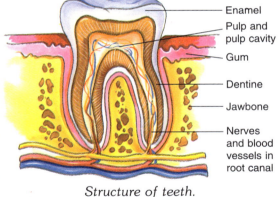
Structure of teeth.

and tight covering around the tooth to protect the inner layers.

Q. What is vaccination?

A. Vaccination is a technique to develop immunity in a person from various dangerous diseases like polio, measles, tetanus, typhoid, diphtheria, etc. Edward Jenner, a British doctor, was the first person to discover vaccine against cowpox. In this process the body is innoculated with the germs of a particular disease. The

Vaccination.

body develops antibodies against those disease causing germs. When the body is infected by these germs again at any other time, the body does not suffer from the disease as it had already developed immunity against it.

Wide spread vaccination programme has almost eradicated smallpox from the whole world. Today, millions of children are innoculated everyday against various diseases.

Q. What is meant by atherosclerosis?

A. Atherosclerosis refers to the condition in which there is a loss of elasticity in the large arteries and a thickening of the arterial walls. The thickening results from deposits called *plaques* composed of cholesterol, calcium, fibrin and other fatty substances which get deposited within the wall of the artery between the smooth muscle and the inner lining. Sometimes they may cause the rupture of the inner lining of the arterial walls causing clot formation leading to heart attacks and strokes.

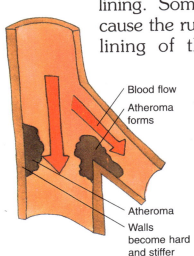

Atherosclerosis.

COMPUTERS AND COMMUNICATION

Q. What is the job of a computer technician?

A. A computer engineer is a specially trained person who repairs all the hardware parts of a computer system. The technicians check the computer parts like peripherals, chips, circuit boards designed and built by the computer engineers for any defect or fault and then repair it. They receive the technical training in technical schools or colleges.

Computer technician.

Q. What is the disk operating system?

A. Disk operating system or DOS is a system in the computer which makes backup copies of the original disks. DOS has many applications. It has its own set of commands which manage and organize the files in the computer. It helps to format and prepare diskettes and in changing disk drives.

Without DOS, it would be difficult to access all the files and information in the computer.

Q. What are Windows in computer terminology?

A. Windows is a program in the computer which organizes and runs the data which is fed to the computer. It is an operating environment which controls and interacts with DOS.

Most of the modern computers like IBM have Windows already installed in them.

Q. What is word processing?

A. Word processing is a type of application software which helps in creating type-written documents like letter or report. It is very easy to use, has the ability to move and copy text, check the spelling, print the document and make changes if required without re-writing. Word processors are user-friendly, i.e., they help you if you get stuck.

The two most commonly used word processing programs are **Microsoft Word** and **Word Perfect**.

Q. What is desktop publishing?

A. Desktop publishing is an application program or software which allows the user to combine both text and graphics on the same page. It is used to create newspapers, newsletters, brochures, catalogues etc.

Text refers to the letters and numbers while graphics are the pictures, shapes, patterns, lines, etc. used to illustrate the text.

The application programs normally used for publishing are Page Maker, Photoshop, Corel Draw, Illustrator, Quark Express, Ventura, etc.

Q. What are bugs in computer terminology?

A. A bug is a programming error. If the programmers make an error while writing software programs then the program will not work producing incorrect results or crashing all together. Crashing of the computer freezes the computer system and it has to be restarted. The computer bug is easier to detect and fix as it is not as destructive as the computer virus.

Q. What is meant by processing?

A. Processing means the manipulation of the data by the computer to transform it into meaningful information. The central processing unit processes the data in the computer. It consists of three parts — the control unit, arithmetic logic unit and the memory unit.

The control unit interprets the data and directs the step by step operation of the computer system.

Arithmetic logic unit performs the mathematical and logical operations. Memory unit stores all the data in the computer.

Q. What is a menu?

A. A menu is an on-screen display listing the options available to the user within a program. A menu bar is present at the top of the

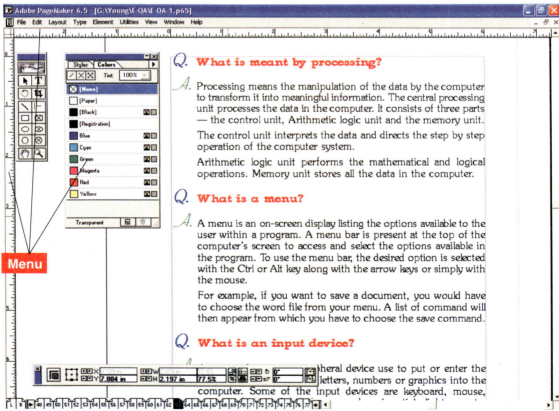

Menu.

computer's screen to access and select the options available in the program. To use the menu bar, the desired option is selected with the Ctrl or Alt key along with the arrow keys or simply with the mouse.

For example, if you want to save a document, you would have to choose the word file from your menu. A list of command will then appear from which you have to choose the save command.

Q. What is an input device?

A. An input device is a peripheral device use to put or enter the information which can be letters, numbers or graphics into the computer. Some of the input devices are keyboard, mouse,

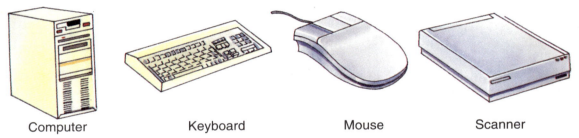

Computer   Keyboard   Mouse   Scanner

Input devices.

scanner, desks and disk drives, modem, joystick, light pen, etc. Each input device has a particular function like the mouse is used to move the cursors or other objects around on the screen while a joystick is used for playing games.

Q. What are output devices?

A. Output devices are peripheral devices that display the output. Some of the output devices are monitor, modem, printer, disks and drives, speakers and speech and

Monitor   Speaker

Output devices.

voice synthesizers. Each output device has a separate function. The screen of the monitor displays words, numbers and graphics while the speakers output the sound and the printer gives a hardcopy of the documents on a paper.

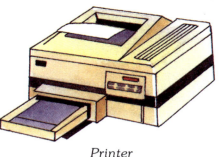
Printer

Q. What is a virus?

A. A virus is a part of software program designed intentionally to sabotage the computer. A computer virus affects the working ability of the computer by attacking other software programs. It can also affect the disks used in an infected computer and spread from the computer to another through them.

The consequences of a virus may be change in the colours on the monitor to total destruction of all the data on the hard drive.

Q. What does ROM stand for?

A. ROM stands for Read Only Memory. A ROM is a permanent memory chip installed in the computer at the time of manufacturing. It cannot be changed or erased when the computer is switched off. ROM tells the computer how to do the various operations like how to turn itself on and off, load the computer's operating system, how to read information from disks, etc.

Q. What is a byte?

A. A byte is a group of eight bits operating together as a single unit. A byte is the amount of information needed to produce an alphanumeric character which may be a letter, a number, a punctuation mark, etc. found on the keys of the keyboard, each having its own pattern of 'ons' and 'offs'. The computer forms words using these bytes. Half a byte is called a *nibble*.

Q. **What is a bit?**

A. A bit is the smallest unit of information that a computer can understand or process. It is formed from binary digits and can be either *1* or *0*.

The information fed into the computer is changed into electronic pulses which the computer can understand. A pulse is either equal to 'on' or 'off'. 1 stands for 'on' and 0 (zero) stands for 'off'. The computer only understands this binary code, uses these two choices to process all kinds of information.

Q. **What are disks?**

A. A disk is a reusable storage device that holds information. It is inserted in the computer's floppy disk drive. It is used to store the finished work of a computer and transport programs from one computer to another.

Disks come in various sizes and with different capabilities. There are two types of disks — magnetic and optical magnetic disks such as floppy disks which are round plastic disks coated with a magnetic substance, optical disks such as CD-ROMs and laser disks which have their data burned into them with a laser.

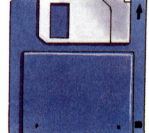

Floppy diskette.

Q. **How should you take care of the disks?**

A. Proper care should be taken of the disks otherwise it will loose all the information it holds.

A disk should never be touched but handled only by its label. It should be kept clean, dry and out of the direct sunlight, heat or freezing temperatures. A disk should not be bent or dropped on the floor. Disks should be kept away from magnetic fields like computer, microwave or T.V., etc. Writing on the disk spoils it. Anything to be written should be written on the label. All the disks should be stored standing upright in their cases.

Q. **Who is a software librarian?**

A. A software librarian is a person who files and stores the disks in an organised system in a software library. Many big organisations which have a lot of software containing data and files employ the software librarians. The only qualification required is a high school certificate and the ability to organise and file.

Q. **Who is a computer sales representative?**

A. A computer sales representative is a person who sells computers to people. He must have a knowledge of the computer products that he is offering to people and should be able to satisfy the

Computer sales representative.

customer's needs with his products. He must have a pleasing personality and good talking skills besides knowledge of computers and technology.

Q. **Who is a systems manager?**

A. A systems manager is a person who supervises the working of a computer system in a business or an organisation. It is his job to ensure the proper functioning of all the computers and to keep abreast with all the new software and hardware developments.

A college graduate in computer science can become a systems manager.

Q. Who is a technical writer?

A. A technical writer is a person who writes the manuals that accompany the newly purchased computers. These manuals inform the buyer how to operate, work and look after the computer. A college graduate with good writing skills and knowledge about electronics and computer can become a technical writer.

Q. Who are computer teachers?

A. Computer teachers are people who teach others how to use computers. They are engaged by schools and organisations to make children and employees computer literate. They also teach the faculty members of an organisation how to select software which would enhance their instruction and curriculum.

Computer teachers should have a diploma or degree in computers besides having teaching credentials.

Computer teacher.

Q. How is language translated by computers?

A. The computers can translate one language into another. The computer memory stores words in one language and their equivalent words in other languages. There are computer programs which can translate a single word to a full sentence in one language to its equivalent in another language.

Q. What is the difference between the Autocad and the Autolisp program?

A. Autocad is a CAD software program used mainly as a drafting tool in engineering and architectural design. Autolisp is a programming language which is utilized to run separate programs within the Autocad environment to customize its various commands and to perform certain specified tasks, thereby making Autocad more user friendly.

Q. Can our brain capacity be measured in bytes?

A. Our brain capacity can not be measured in bytes. The bytes in computer can make the robots perform repetitive tasks but they cannot handle the unexpected tasks for which they have not been programmed. Also, with language, the bytes can generate intelligible sounds and recognise speech patterns. But they cannot understand so much that they are able to take into account the context of words.

That is why it is not possible for bytes to be measured with brain capacity or *vice versa*.

MODERN TECHNOLOGY

Q. **What is a laser?**

A. The word *laser* is actually the short form of Light Amplification by Stimulated Emission of Radiation. A laser is a device that produces an intense beam of coherent monochromatic radiation in the infrared, visible or ultraviolet region of the electromagnetic spectrum, by stimulated emission of photons from an excited source. It strengthens light and produces a narrow beam of light having only one wavelength. The wavelength depends on the material used to make it.

A laser beam is used to check the alignment of a tunnel under construction because laser light does not spread out as ordinary light does.

Lasers are used to carry telephonic conversation, check the alignment of a tunnel under construction, perform delicate operations of human eye, to read bar codes, and so on.

Q. **What is a lathe?**

A. A lathe is a machine for shaping wood, metal, etc. by means of a rotating drive which turns the

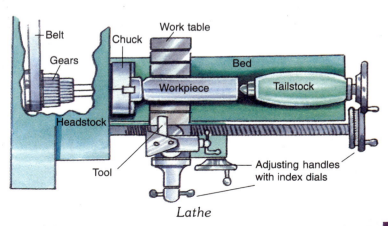

Lathe

piece being worked on against changeable cutting tools. For wood, the tools may be held by hand but for metal the tools are clamped on to a moving platform.

A lathe can be used for drilling, polishing and cutting screw threads into metal rods.

Q. What is liquid crystal display?

A. Liquid crystal display (LCD) is a form of visual display in electronic devices in which the reflectivity of a matrix of liquid crystals changes as a signal is applied. Liquid crystals are materials that flow like a liquid but have a structure like a crystal. A layer of this is laid between two sheets of glass. When electricity is passed

A calculator with LCD display.

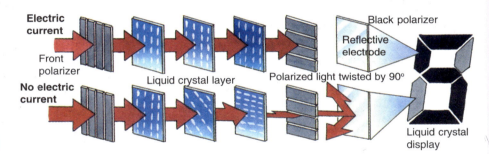

In a LCD, the crystal is between two polarizing filters at right angles to each other, which together block polarized light.

between the two sheets, the crystals block the light making the display opaque. When no current flows, the liquid crystal is clear and transparent.

Liquid crystal display is used in many calculators, watches, flexible thermometers, etc.

Q. What is a loudspeaker?

A. A loudspeaker is an apparatus which converts electrical impulses into sound waves especially music and voice. The sounds we hear on radio, television and cassette recorders all come from loudspeakers.

The loudspeaker has a coil placed between the poles of a magnet and a plastic or paper cone. The electrical signals are fed to the coil causing it to vibrate which in turn makes the cone vibrate. The vibrations of the cone are heard as sound.

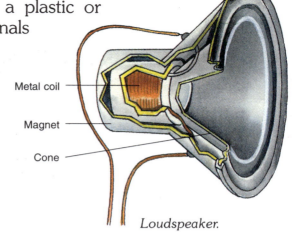

Loudspeaker.

Q. What is magnetic levitation?

A. Magnetic levitation or Maglev is a technique of lifting objects by using the repulsive forces of the magnet. This method has been employed by the Japanese to make an experimental train in 1987 called *MLU-001*. Research still continues for the application of this technique in making future trains.

In this method magnets are laid on the rail track and the powerful motors in the train pushes against them. Initially the magnetic field is such that the train is attracted towards the magnet which makes it to go forward. But then the direction of the

A maglev train is used as a shuttle to carry passengers between the terminals of large airports.

magnetic field is changed so that the magnet and the train repel each other making the train move even faster without touching the rail tracks. Since there is no contact between the train and the track, a lot of energy is saved due to the absence of friction and wear and tear.

MODERN TECHNOLOGY

Q. What is maser?

A. Maser stands for Microwave Amplification by Stimulated Emission of Radiation. It is a device which uses the stimulated emission of radiation by excited atoms to amplify or generate coherent monochromatic electromagnetic radiation in the microwave range. The first maser was made in 1956 at the Bell Laboratories in the United States.

Masers find their use in clocks, amplifiers, satellite communications and radio astronomy.

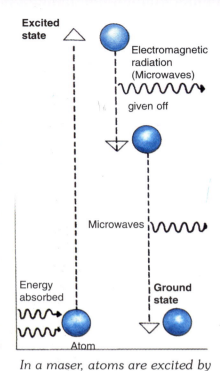

In a maser, atoms are excited by firing bursts of energy at them. These excited atoms loose this energy and return to their ground state in two stages. Microwaves are released as the atom changes from one energy level to the lower one.

Q. What is a microchip?

A. A microchip is a small piece of semiconductor, usually silicon, used to carry electronic circuits. The silicon chip is sealed inside a plastic block with metal contacts along its sides for connecting it to a printed circuit board. The plastic block contains thousands of electronic components which would otherwise occupy a lot of space. Microchips can carry out more than a million operations per second. There are different types of microchips for different works like memory chips store computer data.

Microchip.

Q. What is a microprocessor?

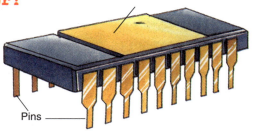

Microprocessor.

A. A microprocessor is an integrated circuit that contains all the functions of a central processing unit of a computer. It was introduced in the early 1970s, by the USA's Intel Corporation. It is made up of a silicon chip integrated circuit which is mounted on a base by two rows of pins. The small size of microprocessors made it possible for microcomputers to come into being. Microprocessors are also used in automatic control systems for various machines.

Q. What is a metal detector?

A. A metal detector is a device used to detect the presence of metals in the ground with the help of radiowaves. It consists of two parts — the detector and the headphones. The detector sends out radio waves into the ground. The non-metallic objects

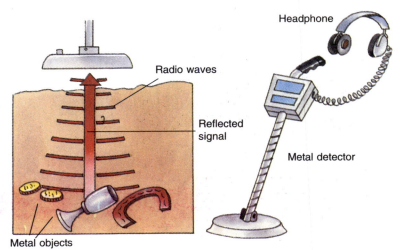

The radio waves reflected by the metal are converted into high-pitched sound in a metal detector.

let the waves pass through them while the metallic objects absorb some of the waves and reflect back the rest. The reflected waves

MODERN TECHNOLOGY

are picked up by the receiving circuit linked to headphones. The frequency of the reflected waves is different and converted into a strong high pitched signal by the circuit indicating the presence of the metal.

Q. What are monoclonal antibodies?

A. Antibodies are blood proteins produced in response to and then counteracting antigens (products of a harmful disease). Monoclonal antibodies are antibodies produced artificially by a single clone

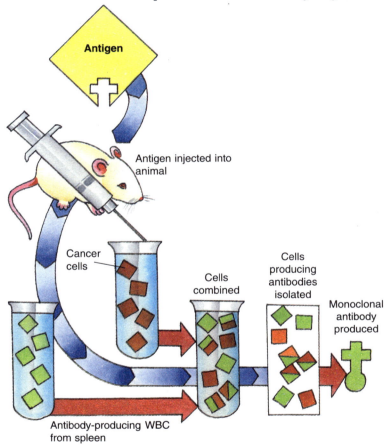

Production of monoclonal antibodies.

and consisting of identical antibody molecules. Large quantities of monoclonal antibodies are produced using hybrids of white blood cells (WBC) and cancer cells. These antibodies are then used for the treatment of diseases.

Q. What is nylon?

A. Nylon is a synthetic polyamide fibre having a protein like structure with tough, light-weight, elastic properties. It was the first synthetic fibre to be developed in the 1930s. It got its name from New York and London as it was simultaneously developed by different scientists in New York and London. It comes in two forms — solid blocks and fibres. The solid form is suitable for making combs, small gear wheels and bearings. The nylon fibres can be woven to make fabrics, socks, etc.

Q. What is a microphone?

A. A microphone is a device for converting sound waves into electrical energy vibrations which may be reconverted into sound after transmission by wire or radio or after recording. Different types of microphones work in different ways. The diaphragm varies with the electromagnetic induction of a coil of wire in a dynamic microphone, electrical resistance of a carbon contact in a carbon microphone, capacitance in the circuit in a condenser microphone and piezoelectric crystal in a crystal microphone. The mouthpiece of a telephone has a microphone in it.

Microphone.

Q. What is a polaroid camera?

A. A polaroid camera is a type of camera with internal processing that produces a finished print rapidly after each exposure. It was invented by Edwin Land in 1948. In the early version of

Polaroid camera.

the polaroid camera, the film was made in two parts. The exposed film had to be kept for one minute and then the two layers were peeled apart to get the photograph. But modern polaroid camera produces a film that develops in daylight on its own.

Q. What is a photocopier?

A. A photocopier is a machine used to produce duplicate copies of a page or document. The technique behind photocopying is called *xerography* which was invented by Chester Carlson in 1937.

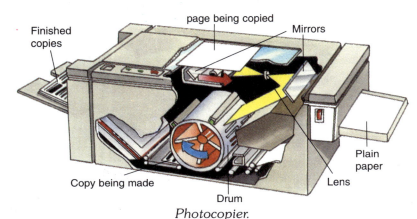
Photocopier.

The machine consists of a drum which is electrified all over and dusted with black powder. When the paper to be copied is kept over a sheet of glass and a bright light shines on it, a bright image of it is focussed on to the charged drum. The electric charge is destroyed whenever the light strikes the plate. The black powder clings on to the electrified parts of the drum from where it comes on to the sheet of paper. The heat makes the image permanent and the sheet of paper comes out as a copy of the page.

Q. What is a prism?

A. A prism is a solid transparent body usually triangular in shape with refracting surfaces at an acute angle with each other. Optical prisms made of glass or plastic can bend light

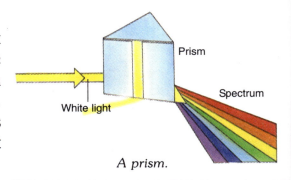
A prism.

rays and also split white light into a spectrum of seven colours. They are used in many optical instruments, camera, etc.

Q. What is a stereoscope?

A. A stereoscope is a device by which two photographs of the same object taken at slightly different angles are viewed together, giving an impression of depth and solidity as in ordinary human vision. It was invented by Charles Wheatstone.

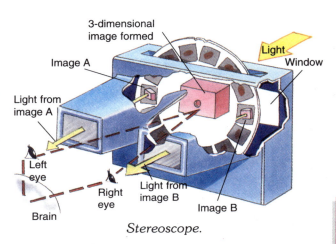

Stereoscope.

Each human eye sees things from a different angle. The difference between the two images called parallax is merged together by the brain to give a 3-dimensional image. Stereoscopic photographs give more information than ordinary ones.

Q. What is a synthesizer?

A. A synthesizer is an electronic musical instrument, especially operated by a keyboard, producing a wide variety of sounds by generating and combining signals of different frequencies. The first synthesizer was made in the 1960s which was very simple. These days digital synthesizers have come which store and reproduce sounds from the same digital code used by the computers. The sounds in the modern synthesizer are made by circuits called *oscillators* which are blended and shaped by other circuits called *filters*. Both of them allow a particular frequency or pitch to be used.

A modern synthesizer.

Q. What is hydroponics?

A. Hydroponics is the process of growing plants without soil in a liquid (water) with added nutrients. A plant requires CO_2 from air and water from soil to carry out photosynthesis. Besides these, it also requires some basic nutrients from the soil like nitrogen, potassium, phosphorus, sodium etc. for its proper growth. In hydroponics, the function of the soil is taken over by the water.

The roots of hydroponically-grown plants are wrapped in polythene.

Many fruits and vegetables have been successfully grown using hydroponics.

Q. What is glass?

A. Glass is a hard, brittle, transparent or translucent shiny substance made by fusing sand, limestone and soda ash. It can be made heat proof or coloured by adding special ingredients. It can be made in different forms like thin fibres, flat sheets, thick castings, etc., or blown into hollow shapes like bottles.

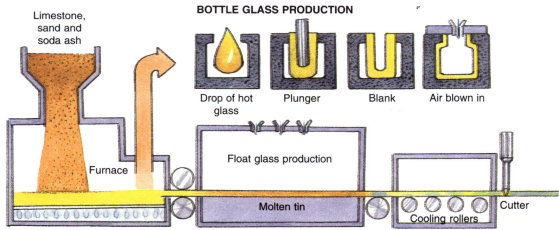
Preparation of glass.

It is used to make bottles, window panes, tumblers, lenses for spectacles, looking glass and also used as electrical insulator.

Q. What is a heat shield?

A. Heat shield is a layer of heat resistant material like carbon and silicon applied on the spacecrafts or rockets to protect them from intense heat. When a spacecraft enters the earth's atmosphere from the space, a lot of heat is generated as a result of friction between the air and the spacecraft. Heat shield protects the spacecraft from these high temperatures and prevents it from melting away. Earlier heat shields were made of materials which could be used only once but now a new type of material has been introduced which can be used again and again.

Q. What is meant by vulcanization of rubber?

A. The process of heating natural rubber with sulphur to improve its properties is called *vulcanization*. It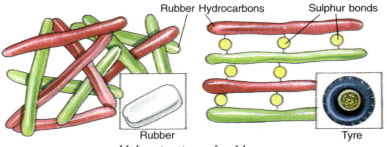

Vulcanization of rubber.

was invented by Charles Goodyear in 1838. Natural rubber is not suitable for most purposes because it is soft and sticky with low strength, elasticity, and resistance to wear and tear. Vulcanization makes it hard, strong, more elastic, non-sticky and resistant to wear and tear. The more the amount of sulphur, the harder the rubber is. Rubber tyres have the maximum amount of sulphur in them while rubber bands have very little sulphur.

Q. Why do different aeroplanes have different wing shapes?

A. Different aeroplanes have different wing shapes according to the roles they are expected to carryout.

Very high speed aeroplanes have short and slubby wings which are swept back to reduce the drag.

Low speed aeroplanes which carry heavy loads have long and narrow wings to produce large amount of lift.

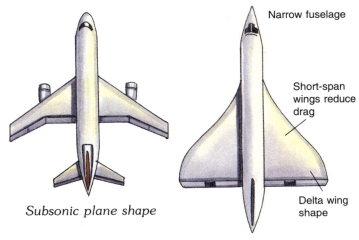

Subsonic plane shape

Supersonic plane shape.

Aircrafts like *Concorde* which can easily travel at high and low speeds have triangular wings with large surface area to provide enough lift at low speeds and sharp backward sweep of the wings to reduce the drag at high speeds.

Q. **What is a humidifier?**

A. A humidifier is a device for adding moisture to air in a room and office. Air conditioning or heating systems can reduce the moisture content of the air so that the people may find difficulty in breathing such dry air. Humidifiers increase the moisture content of the air

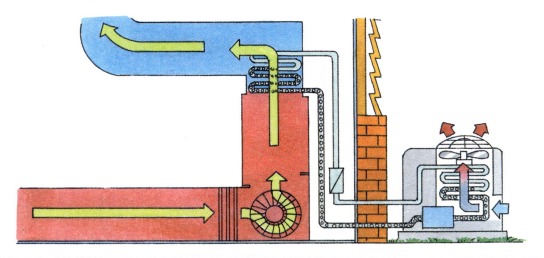

by causing water to evaporate from material having large surface area. In winters, the humidifiers work by reducing the cooling effect of evaporation on the skin. This makes people feel warmer at lower temperatures also.

Q. What is meant by information technology?

A. Information technology refers to the storage, processing and retrieving information through computers. Information of all kinds is stored in computers all over the world and through internet information in one computer can be sent to another computer anywhere in the world. Some shops use information technology in monitoring their stock levels.

Information technology has come in a big way and is here to stay.

Q. What are jet engines?

A. A jet engine is an engine which uses the power of fast moving hot gases for forward thrust. This type of engine is mainly found in aircrafts and are almost error free and less costly than the piston engines. They can carry the aircrafts faster and higher in the air than the piston engines.

Jet engine aircraft.

In a jet engine, air is sucked from the front by a spinning fan. Inside the engine, the air is compressed and burnt with the fuel so that the gases which are produced as a result of combustion are driven out through the tailpipe. The backward moving gases give a forward thrust to the aircraft. There are four main kinds of jet engines : turbofan, turbojet, turboprops and ramjets.

INVENTIONS AND DISCOVERIES

Q. What was Euclid's contribution in the field of mathematics?

A. Euclid was an ancient Greek mathematician who is known as the *father of geometry*. He lived in Alexandria around 300 B.C. and became famous for his books called *Euclid's Elements*. It is a set of 13 volumes containing valuable information on geometry in a logical manner.

His books contain information on various topics in geometry like point, lines, circles, triangles, construction of geometrical figures with the help of algebra, ratio and proportion and their applications.

Q. What were Magdeburg spheres?

A. Magdeburg spheres were the two hollow copper hemispheres which when put together formed a copper sphere 35.5 cm in diameter. They were built by Ottovon Magdeburg, a German physicist, who lived in Magdeburg to demonstrate the power of vacuum before the Emperor Ferdinand III.

In his experiment with these hemispheres, Guericke bound them together with a leather ring dipped in wax solution to make an air tight sphere. The air was pumped out from the inside of this sphere using a vacuum pump. Eight horses were tied to each hemisphere to pull them apart. The horses were unable to do so at first indicating that the atmosphere exerts a pressure inwards on any surface. This is normally not noticed because of the counter balancing outward force of air or fluid inside the surface.

Q. **Who invented the television?**

A. John Logre Baird, a Scottish engineer is credited with the invention of television. He was the first man to successfully transmit a television picture by radio waves and also the first person to transmit pictures across the Atlantic in 1928.

The first crude television set made by Baird consisted of an old tea chest, a cardboard box for packing hats, an electric motor and lenses from bicycle lamps. In his first attempt, he managed to transmit the blurred image of a Maltice cross up to a distance of three yards.

John Logre Baird.

Inspite of ill health and little monetary support, Baird continued his research on television and came up with the colour television in 1928.

Q. **Who manufactured artificial gene in laboratory?**

A. A gene is the basic unit of heredity. Dr. Hargobind Khurana, an Indian scientist manufactured an artificial gene for the first time in his laboratory in the year 1976. Born and brought up in India, Khurana went for his higher studies to England. There, together with his team, Khurana spent nine years of hardwork in building about 207 genes of a bacteria called *Escherichia Coli* in the laboratory. When this artificial gene was inserted in *E. Coli,* it began functioning as the normal gene. This achievement was a major breakthrough in the field of science and paved way for new discoveries in the field of medicine.

For his work on genes, Hargobind Khurana was awarded a Nobel Prize in medicine and physiology which he shared with M.W. Narenberg and R.W. Holley.

Q. Who discovered the neutron?

A. James Chadwick (1891–1974) was a British physicist who discovered the neutron in 1932. He proved with the help of experiments that the nucleus of an atom consists of uncharged or neutral subatomic particles called *neutrons* besides protons and electrons. He also pointed out that the mass of the neutron was approximately equal to the mass of the protons. Chadwick also produced neutrons by bombarding the other atoms by radiation from radioactive isotopes.

James Chadwick.

For his discovery of neutrons, James Chadwick was awarded the Nobel Prize for physics in 1935.

Q. Who discovered the vaccine for smallpox?

A. Edward Jenner (1749–1823), a British doctor, gets the credit for discovering the vaccine for smallpox which saves the lives of millions of people today.

During his medical practice, Jenner observed that dairy maids who had suffered from cowpox disease were immune to smallpox disease. He tested this by performing an experiment. He innoculated a boy with the germs of cowpox taken from the fluid, from a cowpox sore on a dairy maid's finger. The boy suffered from a mild attack of cowpox, Jenner then injected smallpox germs in the boy and found that he was not affected by the disease thus proving that cowpox germs protected the boy from the smallpox.

This started the practice of vaccination against the smallpox disease.

Q. Who proved that lightning is electricity?

A. Benjamin Franklin (1706–1790) was an American politician and scientist who invented the lightning conductor, and also proved through his experiments, that lightning was actually electricity. He flew a kite made of silken cloth during a thunderstorm. An iron wire about one foot long protruded above the kite. The kite was connected to a metal string at the other end of which was a key that Franklin held in his hand. When the lightning struck the wire, it travelled down to the key producing a spark and proving that lightning is electricity.

Benjamin Franklin.

Q. Who invented the lightning conductor?

A. Benjamin Franklin was an American scientist, politician, publisher, printer, and statesman who served the United States of America. His famous experiment with the kite to show that lightning is electricity made him invent the lightning conductor. It is a device which protects tall buildings from lightning.

A lightning conductor is made of a long metal rod of iron or copper. One end of this rod is about 3–4 feet deep, inside the earth and it runs along the entire length of the building with its upper end protruding 6–8 feet above the roof of the building. At the upper end, a one foot long brass wire is fixed. When the lightning strikes, the electrical charge is carried down by the metal rod into the earth and the building is saved from the damaging effects of lightning.

Lightning conductor.

Q. What were Leonardo da Vinci's contributions to science and technology?

A. Leonardo da Vinci (1452–1519) was an Italian artist, scientist, and scholar. He was one of the first Italian painters to work in  oil paint and his famous painting 'The Mona Lisa' is world renowned. The elusive expression on its face still intrigues many a people. He also made thousands of drawings of human bodies, water, plants, animals, etc. He was a great botanist and zoologist and wrote the first standard book on anatomy.

He was a skilled engineer and worked for Italian nobles and the French king. He designed many forts, canals and some of the drawings found in his notebooks also include a helicopter, machine gun and flying machine. He was also an accomplished musician, composer and singer.

In his notebooks, which are full of his thoughts and drawings, entries have been made in a strange way. He wrote his lines from right to left with each letter reversed. It had to be viewed in a mirror for reading. This form of secret writing may have been devised by him because his ideas were centuries ahead of the time and such ideas were not welcome in those days.

The Mona Lisa.

Q. **Who gave the internal structure of an atom?**

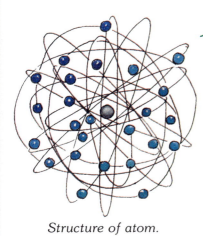

Structure of atom.

A. The mystery of the internal structure of an atom was solved by Lord Rutherford in 1911.

Rutherford conducted some experiments with the alpha rays on the gold foil. On the basis of these experiments, he showed that an atom consists of a tiny nucleus in the centre which is positively charged and contains most of the atom's mass. He also made a model of the nucleus. In 1919, he succeeded in splitting an atom.

Q. **Why did Ernest Rutherford receive a Nobel Prize for chemistry?**

A. Rutherford was awarded the Nobel Prize for chemistry in 1908 for his work on radioactive substances. He discovered that different radioactive substances gave off different types of radioactive rays which he named as alpha, beta and gamma rays. He demonstrated with the help of the experiments that the alpha rays are a stream of positively charged particles.

Lord Rutherford.

He discovered that the atoms of one type are changed into atoms of different types by radioactive decay. On the basis of this, he changed nitrogen into oxygen by bombarding the nitrogen atoms with alpha particles. He became the first person to change one element into another.

Q. **Who invented logarithm method?**

A. John Napier (1550–1617), a Scottish mathematician, invented the logarithm method for carrying out complex mathematical calculations in a simpler way. In this method, complex multiplications are expressed as additions and divisions as subtractions. The exponents on numbers are expressed as logarithm multiplications. After these conversions, the values are obtained from standard logarithm tables and the result is obtained by addition and subtraction. Antilogarithm of this value gives the actual solution to the problem. Napier prepared separate logarithm and antilogarithm tables.

John Napier.

Logarithm method of calculation is still widely used in all parts of the world.

Q. Who invented the system of printing?

A. Johannes Gutenberg was a German scientist who invented the movable type of printing and gave it the first practical use in 1454. Printing made the tedious work of copying the texts and pictures easier and quicker. The forty-two line Bible was Gutenberg's first printed book. About three hundred copies or so of the Bible were printed and sold.

System of printing.

Q. Who invented the germ theory of diseases?

A. Louis Pasteur, a French chemist and biologist developed and proved the germ theory of diseases. He proved that the bacteria and other germs cause diseases. He also noted that the food went bad because of air borne germs. In 1881, he developed vaccines against the diseases anthrax in sheep and later he made vaccines for cholera, rabies,

Louis Pasteur.

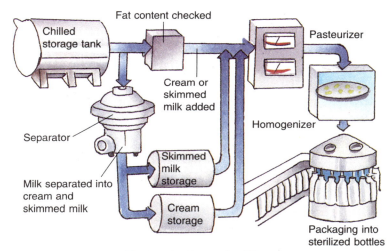

Pasteurization of milk.

and other diseases also. He innoculated the animals and people with the weakened disease causing germs which produced antibodies in their blood. Whenever such people were attacked by these germs again, they did not suffer from the disease as they had already developed immunity against the disease.

Q. Who discovered the law of universal gravitation?

A. The law of universal gravitation was given by Sir Isaac Newton. He was sitting under an apple tree when he saw an apple falling to the ground. This made him wonder why all the things that go up in the air fall down. He deduced that some force is there which attracts all the things to earth. He named this force as gravity and concluded that all the objects in the universe attract each other by the force of gravity. The force of gravity of an object depends upon its weight.

This law explained many unanswered questions. Why did all the bodies fall to the ground? Why did planets revolve around the sun? Why did the planets revolve with different speeds? and so on.

Sir Isaac Newton.

Q. **Who laid the foundation of the modern theory of evolution?**

A. Charles Darwin propounded the theory of evolution and published his work in his book *On the Origin of Species* in 1859. He stated that all the living beings evolved from earlier forms

Australopithecus	Homo habilis	Homo erectus	Neanderthal man	Modern human
1–4 million years ago	1.5–2 million years ago	0.1–1.5 million years ago	35,000–100,000 years ago	Since 100,000 years ago
Africa	Africa	Asia, Africa, Europe	Europe	Worldwide

and that there is a struggle for existence in which only the fittest of the living beings survive. According to him, evolution is a continuous process and that is why there are a great variety of plants and animals.

Q. **Who invented the first astronomical telescope?**

A. Galileo, an Italian scientist, invented the first astronomical telescope and observed craters in the moon, the satellites of Jupiter, sunspots, etc. The four largest satellites of Jupiter are hence known as *Galilean satellites*. His observation through the telescope made him disprove Copernicus's idea that the earth was the centre of the universe. He stated that the earth revolves around the sun and that our milky way is composed of millions of stars. Galileo expressed his ideas in his famous book *Dialogues Concerning the Two Principal Systems of the World*. But the church was critical about his revolutionary ideas and, therefore, put him to prison for his remaining life.

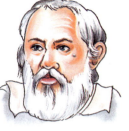
Galileo.

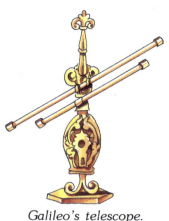
Galileo's telescope.

Q. Who invented the incandescent electric bulb?

A. Thomas Alva Edison invented the first successful electric bulb in 1879. He discovered that the electricity would flow from the bulb's glowing filament onto a metal plate inside the bulb. Such a material had to be found out for the filament which fulfilled the requirements. One which could be made easily and cheaply and could burn for long periods. On 21st October, 1879, a filament made of carbonized sewing thread, mounted in an evacuated glass bulb produced a steady glow nonstop for forty hours.

Thomas Alva Edison.

An electric bulb.

Q. Who invented the phonogram?

A. Thomas Alva Edison invented the first phonogram in 1877. It was hand operated and played recordings made on tin foil cylinders. This first speech recording instrument had a revolving

Phonogram.

INVENTION & DISCOVERIES

tin foil covered cylinder on which mechanical vibrations of a needle attached to a membrane left a permanent impression of the sounds. When the cylinder was rotated with hand, the needle and membranes together acted as a loudspeaker to reproduce the sound.

Q. Who discovered oxygen?

A. Oxygen was discovered by a British chemist, Joseph Priestley, in 1774. However, the gas was named by Antoine Lavoisier. He made the gas by heating an oxide of mercury. A Swedish chemist, Karl Scheele had discovered oxygen two years before but since he did not report his finding, the credit of discovering oxygen goes to Priestley.

Joseph Priestley.

Q. Who discovered the cell?

A. Cells were discovered by an English scientist, Robert Hooke, in 1665. He observed hundreds of small hexagonal compartments arranged in a honeycomb like manner in a thin slice of cork

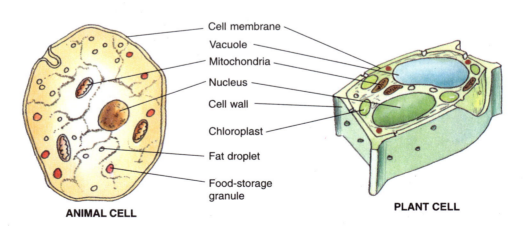

ANIMAL CELL   PLANT CELL

under his crude microscope. He called these tiny compartments as cells and ever since then this term has been in use.

Q. Who propounded the theory of relativity?

A. Albert Einstein propounded the theory of relativity in 1905 out of which came the famous equation **$E = mc^2$**. His theory changed the way of looking at time, space, matter and energy. This theory of relativity actually consisted of two theories—the special theory and the general theory. Special theory states that time appears to pass more slowly on an object that is moving very fast. This effect can be seen in certain subatomic particles which last longer when they move quickly. The shapes of things seen by a person moving quickly will be distorted. The object's length appears to decrease with speed.

Albert Einstein.

The second theory helps us to understand more about gravity, space and nature of the universe. It states that gravity could make light rays bend. Finding out the real position of a distant star from earth would not be accurate as the light rays coming from it have been bent by the sun's gravitational pull.

Q. Who invented the microscope?

A. Anton Van Leeuwenhock, a Dutch scientist, invented the first crude microscope in the 1670s and saw bacteria, yeast cells and blood cells through it. He also showed that fleas hatch from tiny eggs using his microscope. These days powerful electron microscopes can magnify objects upto even two million times.

Anton Van Leeuwenhock.

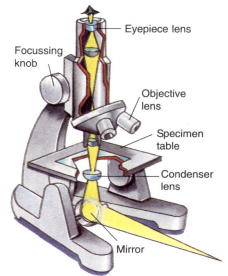
A modern optical microscope.

INVENTION & DISCOVERIES

Q. What is a telescope?

A. A telescope is a scientific instrument which makes distant things look near. It works by focussing the light from an object into a tiny image. This image is then magnified by powerful lenses so that we can see it in close-up. Hans Lippershey made the first telescope using two spectacle lenses. His design inspired Galileo to construct the first astronomical telescope. There are two kinds of telescopes—reflecting telescopes and refracting or lens telescopes. A reflecting telescope uses a large concave mirror to reflect light onto a smaller mirror which directs it through a lens to the eye.

A refracting telescope uses two lenses to focus the rays of light from distant objects.

Telescope.

Binoculars are two lens telescopes fixed together. Most astronomers today work with big reflecting telescopes.

Q. What is Morse Code?

A. Morse Code is a simple way of sending messages through a system of dots and dashes. Each alphabet is represented by its own dot and dash pattern. Messages are transmitted by cable using Morse Code. The telegraph operator possesses a key at one end to send a signal along the wire. A sounder at the other end receives it. A dot is a short signal and a dash is a long signal. Samuel Morse was the inventor of Morse Code and the first official telegraph was sent in 1844.

Samuel Morse.

Morse transmitter.

SCIENCE

Q. Why are three digit numbers dialled before the regular eight digit telephone numbers?

A. The three to five digit numbers dialled before the regular eight digit numbers are the area codes. There are so many telephone connections that even ten million numbers are not enough. To provide more numbers, area codes are used before the eight digit phone numbers. Each area code represents a particular area in that country. Like 011 is the area code for Delhi and 0171 is the area code for Ambala. A person staying in Delhi and another staying in Ambala, both can have the same eight digit numbers without getting their calls mixed up because they have different area codes.

In places where there are a lot of people in a single city only, the city itself may have several area codes.

Q. Why is charcoal a better fuel than wood?

A. Charcoal is a better fuel than wood because it has a higher calorific value than wood. One gram of wood gives 17 kJ of energy while the same mass of charcoal gives 33 kJ. Charcoal is also a clean fuel. It burns without producing smoke and does not pollute air whereas wood produces a lot of smoke on burning. Moreover charcoal is a compact fuel and comparatively easier to handle and use than wood.

Q. What is rusting of iron?

A. Rusting of iron is the formation of a red brown flaky coating on the surface of iron metal when it is exposed to humid air or kept in water. It is an oxidation process in which iron slowly oxidizes by oxygen in air, in the presence of water, to iron oxide and iron hydroxide. Rust is soft and porous and gradually withers off from the surface and the iron below starts rusting. This process continues till it gradually eats up the whole iron object.

Q. How does the water absorbed by the roots in the ground reach the top of very tall trees?

A. A tree absorbs water through its roots which are present under the ground. The water molecules that evaporate from the leaves as a result of transpiration pull the water up. Water travels in tiny tubes that connect the leaves, stem and roots in continuous strands. The system works because the hydrogen bonds connecting the water molecules are stronger than the weight of the water in the tubes. Because of the high cohesive forces between water molecules, it travels as a continuous strand without breaking even for hundred metres.

Q. What is the composition of sunlight?

A. The sunlight is made up of three types of waves—ultraviolet rays, visible light and infrared rays. All these waves have different wavelengths, the ultraviolet rays having the shortest wavelength and the infra red having the longest. Both these are invisible to eyes. Infrared

Composition of sunlight.

rays produce a sensation of heat while ultraviolet rays produce flourescence in certain substances. We see only the visible light whose wavelength ranges from about 4×10^{-7} to 7×10^{-7} metre. It consists of seven different colours—Violet, Indigo, Blue, Green, Yellow, Orange and Red (VIBGYOR).

Q. Why does a steel ball weigh more than an apple of the same size?

A. All the matter present on the earth is made of atoms. Weight of an object depends on the force of gravity with which it is attracted towards the earth and the weight and kind of packing of the atoms making that object.

The atoms of a steel ball are heavier and are closely packed together than the atoms of an apple. Since the gravity pulls harder on denser materials, a steel ball weighs more than an apple of the same size.

Q. How does a junk-yard magnet work?

A. Junkyards have powerful magnets called *electromagnets* attached to huge cranes to separate the metallic waste from the rest of the junk. Electromagnets are made by coiling electrical wire around a bar of iron. When electric current flows through the wire, it creates a magnetic field. The magnetism of both the iron bar and wire coil combine to attract the pieces of metal from the junk. When the operator switches on the magnet and moves it over the junk, the metal pieces stick to it and are moved to other place by swinging the magnet. When the current is switched off, the metal pieces drop off.

Junk-yard magnet

Q. What makes moving things slow down and stop?

A. It is the force of friction which makes moving things slow down and stop. This force is created whenever two things run against each other and friction makes it hard to move something across a surface.

Friction slows down the speed.

Q. How do the scientists make out that the ozone layer is under attack?

A. Spectrophotometer is an instrument which shows how much radiation is getting through the ozone layer and reaching the earth's surface. When it is seen that the amount of ultraviolet radiation is on the rise, a reduction in the amount of ozone in the ozone layer is indicated.

Q. What is the principle behind the working of a television?

A. A television set is the receiving end of the electronic signals transmitted from T.V. stations.

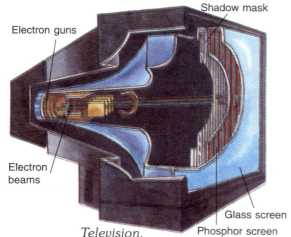

Television.

During a programme in the studio of a T.V. station, the picture and sound are converted into electronic signals. These are amplified and then transmitted as radio waves. The T.V. picks up these waves through the antenna and changes them back into electric signals which pass into the T.V. set as picture and sound.

98

Q. How do hot air balloons fly?

A. Hot air being lighter than cold air rises up in the atmosphere. Hot air balloons use this principle of air. The balloon is attached to a basket which carries people. The basket also has a tank of gas and burner. When the burner is turned on, it heats the air going into the balloon. When the air becomes hot enough, the balloon takes off. The balloon is made of lightweight cloth but doesn't let the hot air escape. When the burner is turned off, the air in the balloon starts cooling, bringing the balloon down.

Hot air balloon.

Q. How is a hot air balloon steered?

A. The hot air balloon does not have any equipment like a steering wheel or stick to steer itself. Its direction can still be controlled to some extent.

The height of the balloon can be controlled by switching the burner

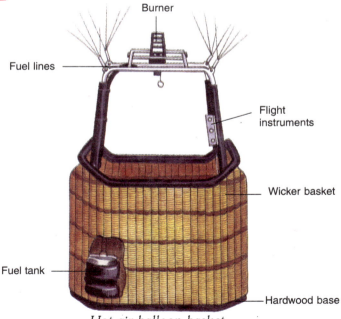

Hot air balloon basket.

on and off. At an 'on' position, the balloon will rise up and *vice versa*. The winds at different heights blow in different directions. After selection of the direction in which you want to go, the balloon can be brought to a height where such a wind is blowing.

Q. What is an echo?

A. When sound waves hit a solid object, some of them go through the object while the rest are bounced back as echo towards the source of the original sound. The echo heard is twice or more louder than the original sound because the sound waves that reach the ears also get bounced off by nearby solid objects. Short and loud noises get the best echoes. Echo-sounders have been of great help to man. A ship's sonar uses echo sounders to find the depth of the sea while fishing trawlers use it to find shoals of fish. Bats use echoes to find their way and prey. Echo-sounders have also been used to map the physical features on the ocean floor. Submarines also use echo-sounder for navigation and direction.

Q. What is an electric fuse?

A. An electric fuse is a safety device for protecting the electric circuits and the people who use them. It is made up of a thin wire which melts at a low temperature inside a glass tube between two metal end-caps. A fuse is placed in the electrical circuit in such a way that electric current must pass through the fuse wire to get from the main power line to the electric wiring in the house. In case the circuit becomes faulty and too much current flows through it, the fuse wire melts and breaks the circuit. Thus it prevents any damage to the circuit which may cause fire.

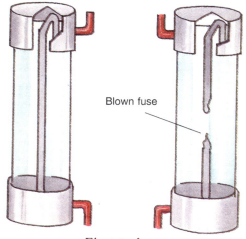

Electric fuse.

Q. Why can't we use a copper wire as a fuse wire?

A. A fuse is a thin wire made of a material like tin or tin-lead alloy having low melting point which melts and breaks off the circuit if the current exceeds the safety limit. A copper wire can not be used as a fuse wire because it has a high melting point. It will not melt easily when a high electric current passes through it and may prove harmful to the appliances attached to it and the user of the appliances.

Q. What is dry ice?

A. Dry ice is solid carbon dioxide. It is prepared by cooling carbon dioxide to a temperature of −78.5°C under high pressure. It should be handled with care as it is so cold that it may cause frostbite. It is used as a coolant in refrigerators and also to produce special effects like fog or steam in television or stage plays as it rapidly changes into gas at room temperature.

Q. Why does a ship float while a small stone sink in the water?

A. Anything that is lighter than water will float on it. The ship is so constructed that it is full of air which keeps it afloat. Air makes it lighter than the surrounding water. Also the ship's body pushes a lot of water beneath it. The displaced water then pushes back up against the ship, holding it up.

On the other hand the weight of a stone is more than the surrounding water as it does not have any air in it to make it light. That is why even a small pebble thrown in water sinks to the bottom.

Q. **How is salt obtained from the sea water?**

A. Salt is obtained from the sea water by letting it flow into coastal ponds or hollows called salt pans and leaving it to evaporate in the heat of the sun. When the water evaporates the salt crystallises out and can be collected. It contains other minerals also such as iodine.

Salt pans.

Q. What is Pasteurization?

A. Pasteurization is the process of killing micro-organisms in food and drinks by heating and then cooling. This process was invented by Louis Pasteur, a French chemist and biologist. The most common use of pasteurization in daily life is the boiling of milk. Pasteurization is widely in use these days because it increases the shelf life of food products and also reduces the occurrence of diseases like diarrhoea etc.

Q. Why is the metal body of electrical appliances earthed?

A. Earthing means connecting the metal case of electrical appliance to the earth at zero potential. Earthing of the electrical appliances is done to save the user from electric shocks and also the appliance from damage due to large currents. If due to some fault the live wire touches the metal casing of an earthed appliance, the current flows to the earth though the earth wire. It does not give the user an electric shock.

Q. What are X-rays?

A. X-rays are electromagnetic waves of very short wavelength and consequently a very high frequency. They were discovered by Wilhelm Roentgen in 1895. X-rays travel in a straight line and are invisible but have a great penetrating power. They leave an image on photographic plate.

X-rays are used by the doctors to detect fractures or defects in bones or teeth. They are also used to study the structures of solids in X-ray diffraction and X-ray astronomy.

Wilhelm Roentgen

Q. Why are X-rays used to study the defects in bones or teeth?

A. X-ray can pass through most of the living tissues except bones and teeth. They can also leave an image on photographic plate. That is why doctors use them to take photographs of

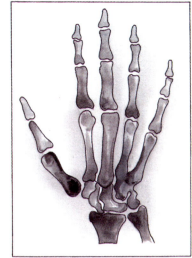

X-ray of hand

the inside of a human body. They give a clear image of the bones and any crack or defect can be easily made out in the X-ray photograph.

Q. Why does a person get hurt when he stops a fast moving ball suddenly?

A. When a fast moving ball is stopped suddenly, its velocity is changed from a high value to zero in a very short time. Due to this its large retardation, the person has to apply a large force to stop it. Since the ball also exerts an equal force on the hand of the person, he may get hurt trying to stop it.

Q. Why is sodium kept under a layer of oil?

A. Sodium is a highly reactive metal reacting vigorously with water to produce sodium hydroxide and hydrogen gas. To prevent its reaction with water, oxygen etc. and to retain it as a pure metal, it is kept under a layer of oil.

Q. Why does a gun recoil when a bullet is fired?

A. When a bullet is fired from a gun, the force which sends the bullet forward is equal to the force sending the gun backward. But since the gun is heavier than the bullet it moves only a little distance and gives a backward jerk to the person holding the gun.

Q. Why does a glass tumbler break when boiling water is poured into it?

A. Glass is a poor conductor of heat. When boiling water is poured into it, the inner walls of the glass become hot and expand. At the same time the outer portion of the glass walls remain cold and do not expand so quickly. Due to this difference in the expansion of the inner and outer walls, a strain is set up in the glass and it breaks.

Q. Why is copper used for making electric wires?

A. Copper is highly ductile i.e. it can be easily drawn into wires. It is also one of the best conductors of electricity and is not attacked by air or water. That is why it is used for making electric wires.

Q. Who was the first man to set foot on the moon?

A. Neil Armstrong was the first man to set foot on the moon on July 20, 1969. He was a part of the Apollo 11 team which

First man on moon.

landed successfully on the moon and explored the surface of the moon on foot and Moon buggies. They took several photographs, performed experiments and brought back rock samples of the moon.

GENERAL KNOWLEDGE

Q. **Why are bananas not refrigerated?**

A. Fruit is a living thing even after it is plucked. It carries out all the metabolic processes which it used to perform while still attached to the parent plant. The shelf life of a fruit can be increased if the rate of these metabolic activities can be reduced. Refrigeration is one such method but the low temperature for each fruit is different below which it receives damages known as chill injury. Banana being highly chill sensitive can be refrigerated at 13^0C. The domestic refrigeration, have a temperature range of about $0-7^0$C and hence the banana cannot be refrigerated in them. But the commercial fruit storage units have the facility of setting and maintaining a desired low temperature where even the banana can be stored.

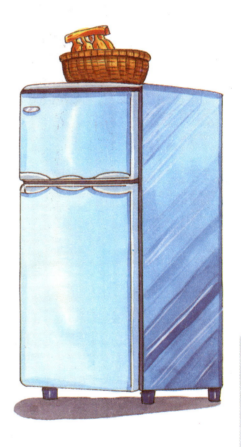

Q. **What are Olympic Games?**

A. Olympic Games is the world's oldest athletics competition held once every four years. The modern Olympic Games began in 1896 in Athens, Greece. The motto of the Games is Citius,

Altius, Fortius meaning swifter, higher and stronger. The Olympic flame is lit at the ancient site of Olympia by the natural rays of the sun reflected off a curved mirror and transported to the venue through a torch relay. Its flag has five interlocking rings on a plain white base representing the five continents - Europe, Asia, Australia, Africa, North and South America. Every time it is held in a different country and athletes from different nations participate in contests like jumping, gymnastics, races, football etc. The winners are awarded with medals. USA has won 833 gold medals, the highest number since the inception of the Olympics.

Q. What is tele-medicine? Is it useful?

A. The daily dose of television that we watch is called tele-medicine. It includes the serials, movies, news and other programmes which we watch daily on the television.

It is useful only if we can get good entertainment and learn new things by watching it.

Q. Which is the most important industry of Assam?

A. Tea is the most important industry of Assam, which contributes 15% of the world's tea production. It has tea gardens occupying an area of about 2.30 lakh hectares. Guwahati tea aAuction centre is the world's biggest centre for CTC tea. Most of the good quality tea produced in Assam is exported to different countries.

Plucking tea leaves.

Q. What does the term paparazzi mean?

A. Paparazzi refers to the photographers who doggedly pursue celebrities with the aim of snapping sensational pictures. This term is derived from Paparazzo, a street photographer in the famous Italian director Federico Fellini's 1960—cult film 'La Dobe Vita'. And of course, nobody can forget the sensational photographs filmed by a paprazzi of late Lady Diana and her boyfriend.

Q. What is an autopsy?

A. Autopsy is the medical examination of the body after death to ascertain the cause of death. It is done by studying the pieces of tissues removed from the body, both microscopically and chemically. There is practically no evidence of autopsy on the body as only very small samples of tissues are taken from the body. Before performing an autopsy permission has to be taken from the nearest relative of the dead.

An autopsy helps to establish the time of death, identify the dead, cause of death and even gives information about the disease from which the dead person suffered that could be helpful in saving the lives of the surviving relatives.

Q. Which was India's first National Park?

A. Corbett National Park established in 1935 was India's first National Park. It covers an area of over 521 sq. km. in the two hill districts of Pauri Garhwal and Nainital and contains over 400 bird species and animals like Elephant, Sambar, Panther, Tiger, Kopard, Barking deer etc. It was first named as Hailey National Park after the Governor of United Provinces which was later on changed to Ramganga National Park in 1952. Finally in 1957 it was renamed Corbett National park.

Q. **What is Mach Number?**

A. Mach Number denotes the ratio of the speed of a body to the speed of sound in a particular medium, usually air. Mach Number was named after the man who invented it, Earnest Mach (1838–1916). If the speed of an aircraft is equal to the speed of the sound, it is said to be flying at Mach 1. Mach 2 means twice the speed of sound and so on. Speeds below Mach 1 are subsonic and those above Mach 1 are supersonic. Speeds above Mach 5 are hypersonic. All passenger airlines are subsonic except Concorde, which flies at speeds above Mach 2. There are supersonic planes which can fly six times the speed of sound.

Earnest Mach.

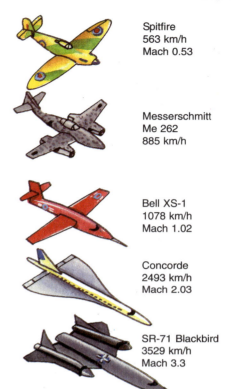

Type of aeroplanes.

Q. **What do you mean by consumer bar code?**

A. It is a combination of thin and thick vertical lines separated by uniform gaps printed on the container of consumer goods. They are read optically by electronic instruments and give vital information regarding the contents like price, size, item description, identification number etc. These bars help in

Consumer bar code.

111

preparation of cash memos electronically and also give vital information regarding available stocks.

Q. What are skyscrapers?

A. A skyscraper is a very tall building of many storeys. At one time, New York was known as the *city of skyscrapers* but now they are built all over the world. The Petronas Twin Towers in Kuala Lumpur (Malaysia) are at present the tallest buildings.

The first skyscraper was built in 1884 in Chicago in USA. Designed by William Le Baron Jenney, it had an iron frame.

In this age when land is at a premium, skyscrapers and other multistoreyed buildings make the best use of land.

Q. Which family has won the maximum number of Nobel Prizes?

A. The Curie family has won the maximum number of Nobel Prizes, a total of five prizes. Two generations of this family have dedicated their life for the development of science.

Marie Curie.

Marie Curie received Nobel Prize twice, one for physics the other for chemistry. Her husband Pierre got the prize once for physics. Their daughter Irene Curie and her husband were jointly awarded the Nobel Prize for chemistry for synthesizing artificial radioactive substances.

Q. What is Koran?

A. The sacred book of Islam is known as the *Koran*. Koran means 'a recitation'. It is a collection of the sayings and preachings of Prophet Mohammed. It has 114 chapters of Arabic verse and preaches that God is one and that all Muslims should be humble, generous, and just. The Muslims believe that the preachings of Prophet Mohammed were the preachings of the God himself and that Koran is a copy of the scroll which exists with the God in heaven.

Q. Which scientist obtained more than 1000 patents in his life?

A. Thomas Alva Edison has more than 1000 patents to his credit, a record which no other scientist has broken till date. Some of his inventions were the incandescent electric bulb, phonograph, kinetoscope, an improved version of Bell's telephone, radio receiver, etc. His name is written in the Hall of Fame among the other famous Americans.

Q. What is a rolling settlement in the stock market?

A. A rolling settlement is a settlement in which trades outstanding at the end of the day have to be settled by making payments for purchases and deliveries for sales at the end of the settlement on the fifth working day.

Q. What is a boomerang?

A. It is a curved flat hardwood missile used by Australian aborigines to kill prey. It is of two kinds. One is heavy and is thrown straight to the target. The other is lighter and shaped in such a way that it is able to return in flight to the thrower.

Boomerang.

Q. What was the Doomsday Book?

A. Doomsday Book was a record of all the property and its owners in England. A great survey went into the making of this book and it was ordered by William, the Conqueror. The survey was completed in 1086. William wanted to find out how much land was owned by the people and whether they were paying the taxes or not. The Doomsday Book contains all the information regarding who owned how much land, how many people worked on the land, how many animals and pastures did they own, how many mills and fish ponds did they have, etc. It was so called because it spared no one and nobody could appeal against it.

Q. **What is the Sphinx?**

A. A Sphinx is actually an imaginary creature originating from the ancient Egyptian folk tales which had the body of a beast, usually a lion and the head of the ruling Pharaoh. A huge Sphinx built by the Egyptians can be seen at Giza, guarding the pyramid of Khafoe. It is 73 m long and above 20 m high.

Sphinx.

Q. **What does 'dating' refer to in the stock market?**

A. Dating is the process in which a financial institution extends a company's line of credit beyond the institution's usual terms. It is often done with companies that have seasonal businesses so that they can continue operating even during the lean months.

Q. What is skydiving?

A. Skydiving is a sport of performing acrobatics under free fall with a parachute. It started in the 1940s and has gained popularity since then. The skydivers jump from an aircraft and fall a long way showing acrobatics before opening their parachutes. They have to steer their parachutes to land on a target marked on the ground.

Skydiving.

Q. What is an abacus?

A. It is a simple counting device with a frame having rows of wires or grooves along which beads can slide. The beads on first wire count as ones, tens on second wire, hundreds on third and so on. It was first used by the ancient Greeks and Romans and is used till date to make the children learn counting.

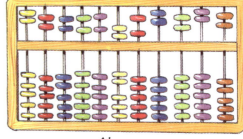
Abacus.

Q. Who produced the first animation film?

A. Winsor McCay of USA showed a series of ten animated films featuring 'Gertie of the Dinosaur' during 1911 to 1921, which pioneered modern animated cartoon films. However, it was Walter Elias Disney who produced the first full length animated film 'Snow White and the Seven Dwarfs' in the year 1937.

Q. **What is NASDAQ?**

A. NASDAQ stands for National Association of Security Dealers Active Quotation. It is the second largest stock exchange in the US, located in New York's Times Square. It is an electronic stock exchange which flashes the stock indices of technology driven and internet based companies on its huge electronic billboard. Two Indian companies listed on NASDAQ are Infosys Technologies and Satyam Infoway.

Q. **What makes the Leaning Tower of Pisa lean?**

Leaning Tower of Pisa.

A. The Leaning Tower of Pisa is a white marble tower 54.5 m high and weighs about 14,150 tonnes. It leans because its foundation is not very strong. For such a high building its foundation is only 3 m deep. In fact, it began to lean almost as soon as its construction was started in 1173 A.D. It took 200 years to build this tower and over the years the top of this building has tilted 5.6 m from the vertical.

Q. **Who was the first scientist?**

A. The world's first scientist was Uddalaka Aruni who lived at least 200 years ago before Thales of Miletus (560 B.C). He understood the laws of nature by observing facts and verifying them using empirical methods. There is a mention of him in the Upnishads.

Q. What are tortillas?

A. Tortilla is the basic food for the majority of Mexicans ever since the time of Aztec Civilization. It is a thin flat pancake made of maize or wheat flour, eaten hot or cold, with or without a filling of meat or cheese. They are also served as enchiladas or rolled tacos covered with a hot sauce.

Q. What is Red Cross?

A. It is an international organization (originally medical) bringing relief to the victims of war or natural disaster. Its headquarter is at Geneva in Switzerland. Its symbol is red cross on a white flag. This organization was founded by Henri Dunant in 1863 after seeing the pain and suffering of the wounded soldiers. Now, it is found in more than 70 countries around the world having different names in some countries. It is known as the *Red Crescent* in some Muslim countries, the Magen David in Israel and so on.

Red Cross does not belong to or favour any country. Its only motto is to help the needy people.

Red Cross　　Red Crescent　　Magen David

Q. What is a Nobel Prize?

A. Named after its patron—Alfred Nobel, a Nobel Prize is a coveted money prize given every year to people who have made exceptional contribution in helping the mankind in different ways.

Three prizes are for inventions in physics, chemistry, medicine and physiology, fourth is for literature, fifth for peace and sixth for economics. Alfred Nobel who invented dynamite in 1867 left $ 9,000,000 for these prizes when he died in 1896. The award money comes from the interest earned every year on this huge amount.

The irony of the whole thing is that the money earned by Alfred Nobel out of the manufacture of explosives is given away for peace prizes!

Alfred Nobel.

Q. **What is a black box?**

A. A black box is a flight data recorder in an aircraft. It records every thing that happens during the flight like radio messages, engine data, etc. It is of great importance because in case of an accident, it is the information recorded in the black box which helps us to find out the cause of the accident. It is a must in all the military aircrafts and modern airliners.

Black box.

Q. **Which great wonder of the world is found in China?**

A. The Great Wall of China is the world's longest wall and one of the great wonders of the world. It is 2,400 km long, 7 m high and has a roadway of 5.5 m running along the top. It was built by the first Chinese emperor, Shih Huang Ti, around 215 B.C.

to keep out the wild Mongol tribes from the north. It stretches from Western China to the Yellow Sea and is made from earth and stone. Watch towers were built every 200 m along it from where the sentries could send warning signals if anyone attacked the wall. Many soldiers, slaves and criminals lost their lives during the construction of this wall. But the wall still could not stop the army of Genghis Khan from invading China.

The Great Wall of China.